CALLED TO BE

Donald Charles Lacy

CALLED TO BE

ISBN 0-89536-340-2   PRINTED IN U.S.A.

Dedicated to

Anne Marie
Donna Jean
Sharon Elizabeth
Martha Elaine

TABLE OF CONTENTS

PREFACE

Called To Be is a preaching/teaching series emerging from the living concerns of a congregation and community, plus my own affirmation that preaching (both verbal and written) is a very special instrument bringing God's grace in touch with human need. The book is intended for clergy and laity alike who are preaching and studying from "The Sermon on the Mount." It can be helpful in both personal and group settings. In a real sense it is a handbook for spiritual growth spoken to, for, and with that vast number of us who know the grace of our Savior and Lord; yet, we have only nibbled away at crusts of bread when we should have been enjoying the riches of the Faith.

Every pastor's study, layperson's bookshelf, and church's library will benefit from this volume. It is an enduring amplification, interpretation, and application of the greatest sermon ever preached.

It is my firm belief that every pastor should be a "resident theologian" who gives primacy to the preaching/teaching function of ministry. Such a servant role is not only essential but sacramental as well. Our laity and certainly our God will not hold us guiltless if we neglect to preach and teach the Word to the utmost of our abilities.

8

CALLED TO BE SELF-FULFILLED
Matthew 5:11-12

The Sermon on the Mount is more than the greatest sermon ever preached.

It is a vibrant account of what discipleship can be at its highest levels. The fifth, sixth, and seventh chapters of Matthew bring before the professing Christian the life that ought to be lived. It can be depicted as a formula for sainthood. Our Lord is saying to those who have already accepted Him, "Look, here is what you are to become." So verse after verse He builds models of conduct. He is not telling us, "Do thus and so and be saved." He is saying, "Since you are my followers, here is the blueprint you need."

It is the **magnum opus** of our Lord's sayings. Even in other religions it has standing. Internationally respected philosophers and social revolutionaries such as Mohandas Gandhi knelt before it. It is said with some authority that to have this single brief writing is all that's necessary to live the Christian life. We are reminded, however, that our Lord did not intend it to be a one, two, three listing of commandments putting man in the same predicament as Jewish laws had tended to do. He is not announcing His way from tablets of stone as Moses had done. He is proclaiming a new life that has already begun in the hearts and minds of His disciples. In fact, Luke tells us the Twelve Apostles were appointed and then Jesus delivered His sermon.

Our Lord says in Matthew 5:11-12, "Blessed are you when men revile you and utter all kinds of evil against you falsely on my account. Rejoice and be glad, for your reward is great in heaven, for so men persecuted the prophets who were before you."

In a sense these are terrifying words, especially in a day when comfort seems to be "the" premium commodity of a good life. Who wants to suffer? "Hardly anyone" is an answer that may even be too generous. Yet, those within the Faith know the profound strength in what our Lord is saying.

"To suffer and to rejoice" appear contradictory. Nevertheless, our Lord puts them together. Christians who have done any growing at all know why they are joined. It has something to do with a very special kind of fulfillment.

II

There is an inviting uniqueness in the call to be self-fulfilled in the context of our Lord's saying. It is a creative selfishness. It signals the destruction of a prideful self and makes way for a divine work of art.

The meaning of the text is pointed out in a suitable series of six.

III

Number one: It is security.

Our Lord wants us to be assured in our on-going battles with evil. There is no life-style so empty as that which brings pain, hardship, and embarrassment and then promises nothing. Jesus is conveying the real picture for the Christian. To be a part of Him and His Way is to meet with all sorts of expected and unexpected punishment. It cannot be any other way in this life. His requirements "of and in love" often meet head on with the powers of darkness. Nevertheless, this will pass and our reward is great in heaven.

The world can never offer such a secure total picture. It can give glitter and glow that for awhile — at least — keeps one on an ego trip down an attractive thoroughfare. In a short time — months or years — a tire is blown, there is brake failure or another vehicle slams into the streamlined "success unlimited." It's all over. There is no assurance hell will be postponed in order for God's grace to have another chance. Those who live for the dissipations of the here and now die discovering the Christians with the torments of evil forces nevertheless have a home prepared for them where there is neither brokenness nor sorrow anymore. Indeed, these two verses from the Sermon on the Mount are security par excellence.

Number two: It is nonsectarian.

There isn't a word, idea, or nuance that suggests a Protestant, Roman Catholic, or some other Christian has sole right to our Lord's saying. Anyone professing His Name can come together around it. There is no admission charge. There is no secret password. There is no "water baptism by one mode only" directive. There is no rigid rule that we believe in a strict understanding what the Lord's Supper is all about. There is no form of church government imposed. Isn't this wonderful! God intends for us to be brothers and sisters in Christ.

There is a universality present, isn't there? Our Lord comes to us with a "here's the way it is" approach with not the slightest suggestion we belong to a particular deonomination or accept a special sect. He doesn't give any indication that the Methodists will suffer more than the Presbyterians, the Baptists, more than the Roman Catholics or vice versa. He doesn't bother with the rewards of a group to which you and I are aligned. Why? Well, I do not presume to know the full mind of Christ. I do believe our Lord never for one minute ever intended for us to be caught up in allegiance to groupings given birth by historical situations to the detriment of His way of life for us. He is attempting to communicate, to all of us professing His name, basically: You are going to suffer because of Me, but be joyful for I will reward you. May God forgive us for the times we have allowed that profound simple truth to go unnoticed! Teach us again and again, dear Lord, Your priorities. Let us remind one another of our community. There is only one Christ who can and does speak with eternal significance. He has spoken and continues to speak through the Word.

Number three: It is serenity.

Would it be possible to estimate the money and energy that have gone into the peace of mind cults over the past hundred years or so? I don't think so. For generations now, someone, about every week or so, has a new handle that will attain the serene life. In the past forty or fifty years, in particular, some gifted guru comes on the scene spraying scents of hope, health and happiness. There is no doubt the public feels a need for such thinking. The sad part, it seems to me, is that all of them — including the most popular — deal with symptoms and never, ever get into the depths of a person where significant change must take place. The promises espoused by such philosophies continually attempt to supply the crown without the cross. Easter is always a great moment, but was and is preceded by Good Friday.

Our Blessed Lord makes the point beyond doubt that we as Christians are going to "take it on the chin" now and then. That's only temporary but it is an actuality. Serentiy is spelled out in accepting this along with the certain reward in heaven. Talk about self-fulfillment! Our Blessed Lord supplies it in the highest and best form.

I once asked a pastor, "Why is there so much unrest in view of the fact our country has the highest standard of living ever known?" He said, "It's because we have been able to live as Christians while we are poor, but we cannot handle affluence." I am not sure I agree, but think about it. Is it possible you and I are looking for the right things but in the wrong places?

Number four: It is single-mindedness.

Christians move along lines that are similar and when there is diversity we are blessed by an over-arching mantel called love that becomes more explicit. Sharing one another's persecutions is expected. Encouragement during times of severe trial is natural. Joy at the death of a saint whose reward is ready and waiting is our rightful reaction. True, we live in a pluralistic society. There are religions and philosophies coming under countless names. It is the day of the supermarkets. Containers, wrappers, and sacks provide differences. The consumer may select one, a few, or many. Yet, the person committed to Christ is bound to others wearing the same yoke. Our Faith is at work in and through innumerable persons and situations. Saint James reminds us early in his initial chapter "For that person must not suppose that a double-minded man, unstable in all his ways, will receive anything from the Lord" (1:7-8).

The tension that we discover between suffering on the one hand and eternal bliss on the other finds expression in spiritual oneness. Like faith and works they go together. Christians are united despite the differing appearances we often see. After all, to be of one mind is not to infer uniformity in organization or identical theological understanding.

Number five: It is solidarity.

To be in harmony with the intention of God for us is to act and react in confidence. It is to know our roots are found in Him. It is to absorb the onslaughts of evil, knowing fully that an indestructable reward is ours. His interests are our interests. His standards are our standards. His objectives are our objectives. Aren't we fortunate to be a part of life like that? It is a case of not always winning but of never giving up. It is a matter of being able to be injured and not suffer spiritual death. Why? We are solidly entrenched in the life-giving stream flowing from the Master.

When we are the weakest, His strength gloriously shines through us. Our powers are found in being perfectly attuned to Him. Saint Paul tells us in II Corinthians 12:9-10: "but he said to me, 'My grace is sufficient for you, for my power is made perfect in weakness.' I will all the more gladly boast of my weaknesses, insults, hardships, persecutions, and calamities; for when I am weak, then I am strong." The world does not know such solidarity. It is foreign in that it proclaims truth which reverses the commonly held measurement of power.

Number six: It is superiority.

The Man of Galilee grants to His followers a superiority given credence in what He has to say to us in the text. Our battles are those that have purpose. They are those that are preliminaries to rewards in heaven. People today are craving to be sold on a solid reason for their lives to continue. They want something that will keep them from falling over the cliff into meaningless existence. Look about you. Many are holding onto life by their fingernails. They don't know where they are going. If they do, quite often they are not sure the destination is worth reaching.

Those who are "born again" understand and appreciate the Master's direct explanation. He does not mislead. He directs us towards the hard facts of being a Christian and at the same time gives us an unobstructed glimpse of the gates of heaven. This is purposeful living at the superior level. There is something for which to live and something for which to die. My, how multitudes ache and groan after such a life! Our Lord says to them "Come to me, all who labor and are heavy laden, and I will give you rest. Take my yoke upon you, and learn from me: for I am gentle and lowly in heart, and you will find rest for your souls" (Matthew 11:28-29). Yes, this is the road to superiority, but it is not as the world understands it.

IV.

The invitation to self-fulfillment has been given. It is given to us in our Lord's picturesque terms. He says, "Blessed are you when men revile you and persecute you and utter all kinds of evil against you falsely on my account. Rejoice and be glad, for your reward is great in heaven, for so men persecuted the prophets who were before you." The guideposts are seen in its being security, non-sectarian, serenity, single-mindedness, solidarity, and superiority.

His message is an "eternal now." The invitation was given twenty centuries ago. It is given today. One is just as valid as the other.

What is our decision? Haven't we been on the surface too long? Isn't it time to travel the road of self-fulfillment with Christ pointing the way?

CALLED TO BE BEACONS
Matthew 5:14-16

I.

For generations, even centuries we have known the significance of beacons.

Some of the first pictures we can remember are those of lighthouses near seashores. They were known to be there to warn sailors that they were near the land, as well as for other reasons. For the light to be out when it was desperately needed was a tragic state of affairs. Ships and boats could come crushing into the rocks and lives be lost. Such structures beaming light in all directions were unmistakably necessary to the safety of human flesh and blood, plus the preservation of costly seacraft and equipment.

Today in an increasingly sophisticated world we quickly recognize the value of a beacon. We may still visualize the stone and sturdy lighthouse on the shores of New England and at the same time know an intricate transmitter is at work in its place guiding aircraft. What we do not question is the necessity of instruments providing safety for precious persons and their conveyances. As a symbol, some kind of beacon represents a caring person or persons and frequently an institution wanting the best for every life it can touch.

Our Blessed Lord says a word abounding with hope and filled with ageless wisdom in Matthew 5:14-16: "You are the light of the world. A city set on a hill cannot be hid. Nor do men light a lamp and put it under a bushel, but on a stand, and it gives light to all in the house. Let your light so shine before men, that they may see your good works and give glory to your Father who is in heaven."

The woman, man, or youth "born anew" is called to be a beacon. Rays of love are to flow from us to a sick and hungry world. Beams of encouragement and support are to be sent to brothers and sisters in Christ. For our light not to shine or shine weakly is to risk catastrophe. The refrain in a hymn of discipleship and witness tells us:

"Let the lower lights be burning!
Send a gleam across the wave!
Some poor fainting, struggling seaman
You may rescue, you may save."

Having made our point that Christ expects us to spread our (His) light let's probe a little further. We ought to be able to do so with real benefit. Our Faith welcomes those who probe in search of greater riches, yes, even more light.

II.

You and I are called to be Christian beacons. Such declaration assumes four things we may never have taken time to consider.

III.

Called to be a Christian beacon **assumes the light to be one.**

What good is a beacon without light? It really isn't useful in any sense, except as a kind of inept ornamentation. It may be the most beautiful piece of equipment in the world. Sometimes large segments of the Church find themselves in this unholy situation. The buildings are big and impressive, but there is little light. The membership roster reads like a who's who, but there is little light. The staff is large, well-paid, and blessed with thorough training, but there is little light. Beacons are made to send light.

Who supplies it? Jesus the Christ is the only answer. He certainly did not call us to be something and then forget or refuse to supply the essential element that gives it worth. If that were the case, our Faith is one that's in vain. The sun set at His death and has not risen since then. We are all in spiritual darkness. Praise God, this is not the case! All of His promises are true.

If Christ supplies the light, then what is our function? Isn't it a matter of being obedient? The person who is bathed in the healing waters of the Great Physician naturally becomes a beacon. The recurring problem is one of staying a beacon. We balk again and again at the dictates of the Holy Spirit. We thwart the light that comes with the new birth. So, in joy and trust, the key is that of being childlike before the throne of grace. Our light will shine . . . if we will let it. Our Lord was not kidding or speaking theoretically when He said, "You are the light of the world." He gives us the very nature of light as opposed to darkness.

Throughout the Church the major source of frustration is the effort to shine light without the prior experience of conversion. The world is a witness to this as well as those within the Faith. There is not enough brilliance in the human mind, heart, and spirit to be a beacon without being called to be one. In short, when we are saved by the grace of God and not of our own doing, we are called to let our light so shine before men that they may see our good works. How great our salvation in fact really is! The Church universally and always suffers because there are those who would attempt to be reputable con-artists, thinking they are doing God's will. Near the end of the Sermon on the Mount He reminds us there will be many on the day of judgment advertising what they did in His name, but He will tell them this in a paraphrase: "Sorry you did not do the will of My Father, depart from Me; you are evildoers."

What next do we find to be assumed?

Called to be a Christian beacon **assumes the strength to spread that light.**

The light of which we are speaking has to be released to be of value. This calls to mind the huge reservoirs that some Christians have. We know it's there. Our spirit bears witness to their spirit. It is as though they are ready to explode with insight, compassion, and joy. Yet, for some reason or another there are no glorious beams; there are only a few glimmers. Christ tells us that just isn't the way it is intended. He doesn't mean, of course, we are to call a press conference with all the media present every time we are ready to witness for Jesus the Christ and proclaim allegiance to His Church. We Christians need to aid and assist one another in bringing out the best. Some of our light may very well be earmarked for another Christian who wants to hide his or her light under a bushel.

There are those maintaining in a loud, articulate voice that the greatest mission for Christians is right here in the U.S.A. I tend to agree with that. At the same time it is important we recognize that work already done over the years. After all the gospel has been preached in our nation in every corner for many years. I have a suspicion much of that mission field is a case of getting those who are already right with their God to begin letting their light shine. As someone has said, "The Christian was never given the Faith in order to be perpetually pregnant." Indeed, we are to give birth! Let's promise ourselves right now to work at mining those diamonds and other precious gems buried in brother and sister Christians.

Obviously the real strength of spreading our light comes from none other than the Master. He will enable us to be individual cities set on a hill. Furthermore, He will make each fellowship of believers a metropolis set on a hill. You would think after observing some people they do not believe the Christ provides the strength built into the very fabric of the text. That is so unfortunate. Let us own Him now! Why evade, bottle-up, inhibit, and disown what is rightfully ours? Hallelujah, you and I are the light of the world! Why not be what we are called to be?

Another assumption awaits us.

Called to be a Christian beacon **assumes the power to capture the hearts and minds of those on whom the light shines.**

To have light and to spread it is all well and good; but how about the power to change, persuade, and influence? We have all seen an attractive, marketable item spread about consumers. Then someone finds out it doesn't have the power to meet needs. Its days are numbered. In a sense the same thing is true of our Faith. It is put to the test. What is not understood by the world is that its power does not rest on the same foundations as a commodity spread before the public. As we say this, we can hear the Master in the Gospel of John 19:36: "Jesus answered, 'My kingship is not of this world. . .'" Those within the Faith know the power of which I am speaking. It is capable of working change at levels where motives become pure and undefiled. When this happens in a decisive way to a person, it may cause the world to label him or her a miserable failure who is both naive and unreasonable. I can think of businessmen at the "top of the heap" - so to speak - who were so overwhelmed by the light of which we are speaking they came tumbling to the ground in the eyes of their ambitious comrades and others of the same syndrome.

Let us never be beguiled by those whose concept and sense of power are diametrically opposed to that of the Master. I believe the Faith is one that is at work in all of life. That does not mean it is welcomed, accepted, or appreciated by those not knowing our

Lord. Our victories are won in love, which usually entails sacrifice and the bravery to say "Thy will be done" in the face of all circumstances. Sadly, some professing His name refuse to learn this. In doing so they bolt the "blessing bin" that wants to give forth luscious fruit. Shame on us for allowing such spiritual inefficiency to take place!

What is our last assumption?

Well, called to be a Christian beacon **assumes the meekness to relinquish the direct impact of such light upon God's call to eternal home.**

The drive to perpetuate goodness may be a legitimate one, except for one snare. Love has a way of eluding the tangible. Those who are beacons in living physical form cannot preserve themselves. It is appointed for us to return to dust. Whatever good we do being beacons must be done during our lifetimes. Therefore, to attempt to manufacture spiritual light beyond the grave tends to be a serious form of sacrilege. Don't misunderstand me! The deceased, especially the Christian dead, are to be remembered and memorialized. This is not the same thing as a deliberate attempt by a Christian to say to others long after he or she is gone, "Look, what a Christian was. There was no greater light than mine." It is a subtle trap, isn't it? We are speaking of one of the seven deadly sins, according to the ancients: pride. This is self-love in its worst form. It is the vainglorious attitude springing forth from the Devil himself. He finds it a temptation of great proportions and infinite possibilities.

Our care and concern we do not switch on or off, but we do come to the place hopefully when we can pray, "Father, I have done my best and I trust my light has aided the bringing into being others long after You have welcomed me home." That's a side to life and death we don't often think about, isn't it? We are to do our good deeds today. Yesterday is gone forever and tomorrow may never come. Tons of money and property cannot guarantee the continuation of our light. In fact, both may be misused to the point of undoing the goodness we have left behind. Now is the time to be a beacon.

IV.

So, we are called to be beacons.

Our Lord is clear, direct, and forthright in His call to you and me: "You are the light of the world. A city set on a hill cannot be hid. Nor do men light a lamp and put it under a bushel, but on a stand, and it gives light to all in the house. Let your light so shine before men, that they may see your good works and give glory to your Father who is in heaven."

The assumptions are fourfold: the light to be one; the strength to spread that light; the power to capture the hearts and minds of those on whom the light shines; and the meekness to relinquish the direct impact of such light upon God's call to an eternal home.

In closing, let's quickly assess our "beacon status." Do we believe our Lord and Savior, Jesus the Christ? Do we need improvement? If so, will we fall to our knees and pray without strings attached: "Lord, be merciful to one who has rejected the call to be a beacon. I promise to do better at this instant."

CALLED TO BE PURE
Matthew 5:21-22

I.

Our Lord is primarily interested in the internal man.

Among His contemporaries this was one characteristic that made Him stand out. He knew it was what went on inside a human being that really counted. External behavior, regardless of how upright it was, could be a matter of discipline and little or no noble intent. His insistence on being born again gave to His ministry a glow and a uniqueness. To force a person to be moral doesn't ever really accomplish much. Certainly there were persons who were epitomies of high moral standards. The Greeks, Romans, and Jews all had their examples. Come to think of it, maybe this was an underlying reason why our Lord was crucified. He brought a religion that made those who felt externally right and proper look internally, and they could not tolerate the darkness. They were "living a lie" and the Christ had the only real answer to rectify their split personalities.

Through the ages as mankind has moved away from the central core of His teaching it has had to return to a singular truth: man's heart, mind, and spirit — his entire inner workings — have to undergo change. This is what every legitimate revival is all about. It is what prompted the Reformation. It is the reason for the Wesleyan movement. The various forms of church renewal in and out of the institution have come into being because of this. Every body of Christian people sooner or later finds it necessary to rediscover the imperative of being purified inside. A reputation for goodness and moral standing rests on shaky legs unless it is born and given incentive from within.

More specifically, our Lord points to a dimension of living that is simultaneously magnificent and difficult.

In Matthew 5:21-22, He says, "You have heard that it was said to the men of old, 'You shall not kill; and whoever kills shall be liable to the judgment.' But I say to you that every one who is angry with his brother shall be liable to judgment; whoever insults his brother shall be liable to the council, and whoever says, 'You fool!' shall be liable to the hell of fire." It is not enough to refrain from killing. It is not right even to be angry, insulting, or call your brother a fool. Our Blessed Lord shows us the purification necessary to be one of His disciples.

So, He steers us away from the fringes and externals that may be mere trappings. As His followers, the call is unmistakable. We are called to be pure.

II.

Called to be pure is to let love have its way. Specifically, this is spelled out in five major ways.

III.

The ability to turn the other cheek in love is the first way.

It is a matter of Christ working through us which makes this happen. He empowers us to do that which He calls us to be. It is not of our own doing. It is the transformation. He works through us. Shout His praises, this can and does happen! Sing songs of joy toward the heavens ... and to one another for the proof of His promises.

Christians are not doormats, but they are so cleansed inwardly they can and do absorb and redirect hate energies. This has been the case since

Our Lord walked the earth. It is no different today. There are those who will ignore, undercut, and even attempt to destroy us. The Faith, wherever lived in a vibrant fashion, has invariably confronted such unpleasant harassment and viperous hypocrisy. The real test comes when we are expected to receive the hateful and sometimes horrendous attacks of those professing His Name. In short, how is it possible for one called to be pure to press for the destruction of a brother or sister in Christ likewise called to be pure? Never underestimate the wiles of the devil! As one kindly, elderly district executive once told me: "I never knew the saints could be so mean until I entered the superintendency."

Jesus prods us with grace to be like Him. I suppose it would have been possible for Him to run away and hide or even leave His homeland to avoid turning the other cheek. He didn't. Our purity is found in not running. However, it is found neither in open display of bravery just to prove a point nor in fanatical aggressive movements in an effort to overpower the devil. Our purity is evidenced at the moment under the Lordship of the Christ. His presence in us makes all the difference.

The confidence to speak the truth in love is the second way.

Christians are often delineated by the world as milquetoasts or well-intended weaklings. Their perceptions tell them we mean well but are not the real movers and shakers in a community. How can those untouched by Christ think any other way? I don't know that you and I should expect anything else. From our perspectives within the Faith, a great many things seem to get moved that don't need moving and shaken when they don't need shaking. We are too apologetic at times. Christ didn't tell His followers to apologize for being Christians. Our confidence to speak the truth in love is discovered simply by being what we are called to be and that means purity in our innermost being.

"The truth never hurt anyone" is a cliche with mixed messages. Christians understand that, in the long run, to speak the truth is not optional but necessary. They also understand their Lord grants to them a confident air which is one of the gifts of being in Christ. Our responsibility is clear. If those who are the recipients of truth disregard, disclaim, and disown it, that's their problem. Hell was created for those who are disobedient to light. This all began with Satan and his crowd.

We must be careful to move in harmony with Christ's Spirit. There is nothing quite so disastrous as a Christian far off-base being cut down by a good throw from the catcher. That doesn't mean we are to succumb to the world's definition of success and failure. No one knows better or feels more keenly than the Christian whether or not he or she is in fact confidently speaking the truth in love.

The honesty to admit mistakes in love is the third way.

It's so beautifully refreshing and creatively revealing to admit, "Well, I blew it" or some other similar expression. I am drawn to people like that, aren't you? Despite what you and I may at first think, this is a method of witnessing to others. Everyone in the Faith can have a good laugh or cry and move on as growing, maturing Christians. The world — at least some will say — "Those Christians aren't so uptight about their righteousness after all. Maybe their Christ is One who tolerates sinners." Our Lord "blew the cover" of some very pious and meticulously upright people centuries ago. They thought a right relationship to God was primarily dependent on keeping score of morals attained and rules obeyed. Failure may be the only way to draw others to the validity of the Faith.

A word of caution: Don't allow the world to be the final determinant of whether or not you have made a mistake. The devil can lead us astray through our own goodness. Accountability to God through Christ and service to others are always in the pattern. Life becomes the most hectically negative at the time Christians lean on the world's definition of mistakes. No person or institution can take from us that all-important, blessed relationship that is our destiny. There are those in the world who will tell us it was a mistake for us to be born in the first place.

"I love you" are the three of the most precious and lofty words you and I will ever hear. It just may be that the only way a brother or sister in the fellowship of believers will ever count you and me as a comrade is as he or she owns up to a mistake and for us to say, "I love you." I like the expression "I love you — warts and all." Whether I say it to you or you say it to me, the message is one of blessed acceptance: I accept you and you accept me. Blessed be the name of our Lord and Savior, Jesus the Christ.

The humility to ask for forgiveness in love is the fourth way.

Christians, especially those in leadership roles, are not to be weaklings perambulating on all fours, but we are to be humble. Sometimes we seem to walk a tightrope. We cannot be running about giving leadership to this and that in the Church projecting weakness. We are not to grovel. We are not to fake competence, because sooner or later we are found out. However, our Lord wants us to be convinced it takes a humble attitude willing to ask for forgiveness in order to fulfill our calling to be pure.

You and I are not exempt from the spiritual law emphasizing even those safely within the fold are to seek forgiveness on bended knees. Assuredly, this is one of the things the new birth teaches us right away. We may soar through the heavenly breezes with joyous dexterity. There come times when we are to repent. This nearly always takes the form of a dual asking. For to be out of harmony with God is to be in a fix with man and hurting. The remedy is forgiveness, but we are to seek it. The willingness to knock on the door of God's mercy and that of man is more than half the battle. God will and does forgive. If the man, woman, or youth refuses to forgive, we enter a period of special dependence on Christ to supply direction. We may not need to ask again and again. Our Lord may release us and leave the burden with the one whose life may soon be blighted because of exercising a closed and negative attitude.

The drive to want to be a growing Christian in love is the fifth way.

Our Lord gives us a Faith with a built-in growth potential. I suppose one can sense this in every recorded word of Jesus. To become a Christian is to be put in touch with spiritual forces conducive to growth. We deny such forces at our own peril. To let love have its way is nothing more or less than to be a growing Christian. The washing away of the impurities on the inside and the replacement of them with purity is a matter-of-fact occurrence for those experiencing it. We should not be astonished it happens. Better still, we should expect it to happen.

To live in the channels of grace provided by Him is a growing adventure. It is stimulated by the call to be pure. These channels are not what we always expect. There are some spectacular and very special surprises. Praise God, there is seldom a dull moment in the Faith of one born again! The Christian is aware that every day is a great day to be alive, and I do not mean a continual parade of the novel and bizarre every twenty-four hours. Ours is an optimism that ultimately never gives way to any happening including death. Our Lord conquered even that and promises the same for us.

Yes, sometimes we get the impression that an individual's experience with the Christ is frozen, fixed, and finalized. I doubt this impression is inaccurate in reality in many cases. It is more than a shame. It is an affront to the Christ who calls him to be growing in love. What will it take to thaw, untie, and make viable some professing His name? One excellent answer is to keep reminding them by various means in love that Christ's call is not to the rocking chair, the affluent but unproductive castle, and the morbidness that comes with potential goodness rotting before our very eyes. Those professing His Blessed Name are the Body of Christ or the Church, a living and ever-growing organism to whom He gave and continues to give Himself.

IV.

Indeed, you and I are called to be pure.

The Gospel of Matthew relates: "You have heard that it was said to the men of old, 'You shall not kill; and whoever kills shall be liable to the judgment.' But I say to you that every one who is angry with his brother shall be liable to judgment; whoever insults his brother shall be liable to the council, and whoever says, 'You fool!' shall be liable to the hell of fire."

It is a call to let love have its way and spelled out in particulars it means: the ability to turn the other cheek; the confidence to speak the truth; the honesty to admit mistakes; the humility to ask for forgiveness; and the drive to want to be a growing Christian.

You and I have accepted Him and now He calls us to be pure. Why tarry? Why even question the proper timing? The call is as transparently clear as the virgin streams of water in the Himalaya Mountains.

CALLED TO BE UNCOMPLICATED
Matthew 5:33-37

I.

When we become overly-complicated, it seems low points in our Faith are reached.

The institutional Chruch suffers as the professionals make the Faith of Jesus the Christ solely into theological dogmas and ecclesiastical intricacies. While we are not to separate ourselves from those in other segments of the Faith, we do know Roman Catholics have gone through periods that are best described as being dominated by the "religion of the priests." The same comment can be made about the Church of England and the several bodies of Orthodox. It seems the Faith is carted off away from the people and placed in vaults seldom penetrated. Power and greed most often seem to be the causes. After all, if you and I have access to educational privileges and structures of influence others do not, it is rather easy to see what can take place. Praise God, from time to time He directly moves on the scene and breaks through the granite of religious exclusiveness.

I do not want to leave the impression there is not need for serious study and organizational know-how among the professionals. Throughout the history of the Church some have been set aside to spend full-time in the ministry. That's right, proper, and necessary. However, there is always the temptation to love the academic world so much and be fascinated by administration to the point the laity may be only cogs in a religious machine. Praise God the Church Universal continues to value highly the general practitioner among the professionals or the local pastor! It is at the level of interaction between pastor and people that the Church comes alive with effectiveness.

Our Blessed Lord reveals a gem of simplicity.

In Matthew 5:33-37 is recorded: "Again you have heard that it was said to the men of old, 'You shall not swear falsely, but shall perform to the Lord what you have sworn.' But I say to you, do not swear at all, either by heaven, for it is the throne of God, or by the earth, for it is his footstool, or by Jerusalem, for it is the city of the great King. And do not swear by your head, for you cannot make one hair white or black. Let what you say be simply 'Yes' or 'No;' anything more than this comes from evil." He is saying in His inimitable fashion, "Don't get caught up in a series of do's and don'ts that require continual explaining and defending." This was a creative move away from the harshness and rigidity found in large doses among the Jews.

You and I today are the beneficiaries of such an uncomplicated approach to God and our fellows.

II.

Called to be uncomplicated points first and foremost to the practical expression of our Faith.

Really ours is a simple affirmation of what it means to be a Christian as our Churchmanship weaves an inspiring fabric.

Seven was and is considered a sacred number. It serves to spell out our call to be uncomplicated. Will you join me as we affirm such a Faith?

III.

First, **we believe in public and private prayer.**

What was man's initial act of worship? In all likelihood it was prayer. It takes no formal training or special location. In fact, man may pray knowing neither how to read nor write. It is the elementary response to the Creator.

In our Faith we pray together to show our oneness in Christ. Many words and feelings can be expressed in a setting cutting across all denominational lines and sectarian groupings. We do not have to be caught up in all sorts of correct religious jargon in order to discover this is a healing and wholesome adventure. To repeat together a child's prayer may be sufficient. The Lord's Prayer continues to be our model. It says it all. The opening lines alone provide the essential mind-set and spiritual tone for a body of believers to send ten thousand devils running for cover. Hear them: "Our Father, who art in heaven, hallowed be Thy name. Thy Kingdom come, Thy will be done on earth as it is in heaven."

Have you met God today in your private sanctuary? Our Lord tells us to go to our secret rooms and pray. One of the earliest voices I can remember over the radio was a lady singing, "Ere you left your room this morning, did you think to pray?" That just isn't at all complicated, is it? In blessed solitary communion with Him we may not utter a word. We may only shed tears of joy and/or sadness. He understands.

Second, **we believe in congregational and individual worship.**

Disciples of Jesus the Christ are to worship together. That isn't very complicated either, is it? It has been true since the beginning. The Book of Hebrews reminds us: "Let us hold fast the confession of our hope without wavering, for he who promised is faithful; and let us consider how to stir up one another to love and good works, **not neglecting to meet together,** as is the habit of some, but encouraging one another, and all the more as you see the Day drawing near" (10:23-25). Participation is the key in coming together congregationally. Too often we have been weakened unnecessarily by "spectatoritis." While the sermon requires listening by the laity, it is nevertheless an activity-opening dialogue between preacher and people.

The Lord's Supper or whatever we choose to name this event is at the top of the scale in what we do together. This was much in evidence in the First Century Church. It, like no other service, is meant for depth involvement by all. The Holy Communion is just not for those "looking on."

It would be to follow a well-worn road to say there is great defaulting in the practice of individual worship. You and I know this appears to be the case. Yet, I have been caught in amazement at times by the spiritual awareness of those I thought never worshiped even in the privacy of their own homes. There are many worshipers, praise God, enjoying Him alone in a blessed one-on-one encounter!

Third, **we believe in group and personal study.**

At the top of the list of resources is the Holy Bible. It is the Word of God. Every Christian or body of Christians has found that, if you get too far from it, you will enfeeble and in time demolish your Faith. United Methodists have gone on record for generations proclaiming that the Christian Faith is received and professed in the Scriptures of the Old and New Testaments. John Wesley was known as a man of "one book." It is to be studied like no other. Today's smorgasbord of excellent Bibles makes us privileged. The interacting in a group with a sharing of ideas and competent leadership is profitable. Alone before one's Bible in serious and reverent study sometimes is the apex of spiritual consciousness. Some of our fathers and grandfathers — yes, our mothers and grandmothers — shed tears of joy and shouted praises to God during those moments. Years ago a small boy passed his grandfather's study and heard quite a commotion of sounds. He told his grandmother he was worried and she had better do some checking. She smiled and said, "Oh, he's fine. He's just studying the Bible." God forgive us in our frequent damnable, cynical, and wretched arrogance for allowing our Faith to be cut to a few trickles when it is meant to be a majestic and mighty waterfall!

Every educational enterprise of the Church is in reality an emerging from the Holy Book. Jesus the Christ is the foundation of our Faith. Yet, we cannot know Him fully, except through the Word of God. The liberal who disregards the authority and validity of it will either return to the roots of the Faith which it provides or will eventually suffer spiritual death.

Now, we are not to stick our heads in the sand and be guilty of bibliolatry or "worship of the book." This would exclude many volumes of great literature and cause us to lose touch with contemporary skills. We are to worship God through the Christ. I firmly believe that when Christians come before the open Bible as a group or individually to receive and be taught, divisive differences fade away in charity and that doesn't imply exacting theological unanimity.

Fourth, **we believe in tithing.**

There are no great churches who fail to practice ten percent giving. Much of today's growth among conservative evangelical Christians can be traced to this uncomplicated mode of sharing. For us to be more than we are as a church it is clear the direction our giving habits must take. While fiscal responsibility is just good common sense, it must never be interpreted to mean stinginess in the Body of Christ.

To penetrate a person's pocketbook and bank account at the ten percent level is to enter into a cherished portion of that person. I suspect more potentially great Christians have lost their way by refusing to tithe than anything else. When the inspiration to do so is there, a denial to acknowledge such a motivation and put it into practice usually makes for unnecessary misery and obvious missed opportunities in the Faith.

Fifth, **we believe in service.**

While regular attendance and tithing are major ways we measure the progressive or regressive moments of the Church, we dare not label service an inconsequential matter. So much of the work of the Church through the ages has been done by volunteers. In fact, I like to think most of it has. Any professional worth his or her salt knows how dependent he or she is upon those giving their time, talent, and energy. Administration in the life of the institutional Church is always significant. The professional who is successful is strongly supported by an army of voluntary workers.

A pastor, now retired, used to say the best appointment is one where everyone has been used to having a job. I think he was and is right. One of the best channels for large numbers of laity to be involved is through a strong liturgist program. In a year's time literally dozens of different lay persons can feel the responsibility and know the importance of assisting in public worship.

Sixth, **we believe in the Church Universal.**

To share our lives with those in other denominations in formal and informal settings is an imperative. Other Christians and their ways are not nearly as complicated as some clergy and laity would have us believe. Too long we have been scandalously separated. We can say, from the beginning, each Apostle gave impetus to a denomination by his distinct relationship to Christ. There is truth to that. Praise God that's not the most important part of the story! Christ is the Head of the Church and they gained their life from Him just as you and I do.

I submit to you the strong conviction that we are expected to visit and share in the lives of Christians, regardless of the label history may have tacked on them. When we go on vacation or feel the need of variety, let's visit the UCCs, Presbyterians, Baptists, Disciples, Lutherans, Catholics, etc. They have great assets given to them by a great Lord. We may need to learn from them something not present in United Methodism. The mission of the Church is crystallized as Christians work, worship, and pray together.

Seventh, **we believe in eternal life.**

Well, we saved the best for last, didn't we? To be in a right relationship with God through His Son is to know a glorious place is prepared for us. The first two verses in John 14 give us all the word we really need: "Let not your hearts be troubled; believe in God, believe also in me. In my Father's house are many rooms; if it were not so, would I have told you that I go to prepare a place for you?"

To know that we are going to be with Him beyond this life is the most uncomplicated abiding truth given to us as Christians. We are His and He is ours; when you and I are safely in the Fold, nothing else matters and yet everything else matters. Just to be with Him is all the assurance we need.

IV.

So, you and I are called to be uncomplicated.

Our Blessed Redeemer and Lord tells us: "Again you have heard that it was said to the men of old, 'You shall not swear falsely, but shall perform to the Lord what you have sworn.' But I say to you, do not swear at all, either by heaven, for it is the throne of God, or by the earth, for it is his footstool, or by Jerusalem, for it is the city of the great King, and do not swear by your head, for you cannot make one hair white or black. Let what you say be simply 'Yes' or 'No;' anything more than this comes from evil."

It is a call articulated in seven simple affirmations: we believe in public and private prayer, congregational and individual worship, group and personal study, tithing, service, the Church Universal, and eternal life.

If we have not done so, let's get with it!

If ours is a partial and/or half-hearted expression of the Faith, let's remedy the situation **now.**

CALLED TO BE HUMBLE
Matthew 5:38-42

I.

Is it possible to meet Christ's requirements of humility?

That's an age-old inquiry. The Apostles fumbled, floundered, and fought with it. Their pride managed to blind them again and again. Saint Augustine wrestled with it. Largely through the prayers of a saintly mother, Monica, he came to terms with the requirement. Saint Francis of Assisi's prayer proclaimed by the ages is in reality a basic plea for us to be humble. Recall, he says, "where there is hatred, let us sow love; where there is doubt, faith; where there is despair, hope; where there is darkness, light; where there is sadness, joy . . ." Martin Luther, that often adamant disciple, gave way to it only after prolonged battles with His Lord. John Calvin, the small, sickly, and exceedingly brilliant reformer, faced moments when his mind and heart were not only fixed and cold but even cruel. Our own John Wesley was not above prideful times that disrupted his relationship to His Lord. E. Stanley Jones with his remarkable spiritual sensitivity battled the desire to deify one E. Stanley Jones. A man still upon the scene, Bishop Fulton J. Sheen, has said in **The Power of Love:** "Pride is the king of vices; it has as its cortege all the other vices. It is the first of the pallbearers of the soul; the root of all evil. Other vices destroy only their opposite virtues, as wantonness destroys chastity; greed destroys temperance; anger destroys gentleness; but pride destroys all virtues."*

In our depths we Christians know we are called to be humble. Christ was and is our example. Are we above him? God forbid!

*The Power of Love by Fulton Sheen, published by Mace Magazine Corporation, 757 Third Avenue, New York, New York 10017. Copyright 1964.

Our Blessed Lord presents to us a scary standard.
In Matthew 5:38-42 His remarks are unforgettable: "You have heard that it was said, 'An eye for an eye, and a tooth for a tooth.' But I say to you, do not resist one who is evil. But if anyone strikes you on the right cheek, turn to him the other also; and if any one would sue you and take your coat, let him have your cloak as well; and if anyone forces you to go one mile, go with him two miles. Give to him who begs from you, and do not refuse him who would borrow from you." Wow! You and I like some of today's youth, feel like responding: "Jesus, you have to be kidding." Of course, He isn't.

Every generation of Christians has had to confront this passage because it comes from the very heart of the Faith.

II.

In our call to be humble, what are our honest reactions?

It seems to me they divide themselves into four fairly easily definable categories.

III.

"This isn't workable" is the first reaction.

If we had a secret device that would record the thoughts and feelings of the average Church member, what would we discover? In relationship to our theme, I'm convinced there would be a great deal of respect for Jesus' words but little seriousness in regard to their practicality. Maybe this is a little like the Episcopal cleric who recently said we give our Bishops a lot of respect but little power. It is never easy to survey or poll religious ideas and feelings. The reason is obvious: this is a very tender and sometimes secluded part of our personalities. Yet, we can say with some certainty many and perhaps a majority of those united with the Church live out their lives largely ignoring our Lord's word on humility. It is not that they (or should we say "we") are bad people who have gone the route of paganism. It is that the call to be humble is just not accepted as a practicality. Of course, that does not change our Lord's word to us.

Now, why is it there is such widespread response of which we are speaking: The world presses in upon us and we do not have the faith to move up into such a realm. That seems to be the cardinal answer. We are held down by a world that is, by-and-large, not Christian. Is this a valid excuse? It's probably the best one we have. While we do not want or need to be too hard on ourselves, to admit openly and without reservation why we are not what we are called to be is therapeutic; this should increase the possibility for us — at least — to attempt the road Christ lays out before us.

Have we ever considered that the crucifixion of Christ takes place many times in our own lives? Perhaps the most humiliating thing that could hapen to Him was to be placed on a cross between two thieves with those who opposed Him shouting slurs and obscenities and His own followers running for cover.

Yet, isn't this what happens repeatedly in my life and your life? We accept Him, but with the restrictions that we are not to be made uncomfortable and sacrificial in any meaningful way. Opportunities come to live up to our calling and we refuse them. We have nailed Him to the Cross! If Christ were to say to His Father, "Enough, I have been crucified for the last time," in what sort of universe would we find ourselves? Isn't that what the Second Coming is all about? I believe it is. Someday our Blessed Lord will shout throughout the heavens, "Enough!" Indeed, to put it into a colloquialism: "the ball game will be over."

It's time to move ahead.

"It may be workable, but it will make us into jellyfishes" is the second reaction.

We cannot justify it in terms of what it will do to us. There are visions of becoming spineless creatures begging just to breathe fresh air, eat bread, drink water, and walk the earth. We maintain that no one can live the way Jesus suggests and maintain a healthy self-image. Who ever heard of a person bowing and scraping in such a fashion? This must be a mistake the Bible translators have not been able to handle. Any reasonable human being knows such a style of living will make one into a laughingstock. Who wants to be that? That kind of ridicule isn't expected of us.

The world communicates to us, in ways too numerous to mention, the ludicrous and devastating hazards in giving it a try. We look at the prospect of being less than fully adult, not insisting on our rights. What sort of asininity is this anyway? Are we to be subjected to demands that prohibit complete personhood? The world taunts us by emphasizing again and again that it's such a shame we have to let a book tell us that we are — in effect — to live on our knees. There isn't much to life and to spend it in joyless moments of subjection is the height of ignorance, we are told. What can you and I say to this? Aren't we largely in agreement with it? Aren't we just real happy to accept Jesus the Christ and let well enough alone? Well, I don't relish being pictured as a jellyfish, do you? After all, man was created to walk upright and not crawl on his belly.

The world constantly batters and bruises us with images of the absurd following from our obedience to the Man of Galilee. It admits oftentimes to the possibility of our Lord's words being put into practice. But at what a price! We buy that suggestion and do so with hardly a whimper. We would rather save face by balancing our Lord's call over against the world's call and end up by rationalizing our way into believing our Lord meant well but He really didn't mean what He said. Then we are left with the most satanic inquiry of all: just what parts of the Sermon on the Mount are inspired and applicable today?

We must not tarry.

"It is workable only for those willing to live a cloistered life" is the third reaction.

That sounds good and lets us off the hook. I guess the best feature to this reaction is that we can subconsciously delegate the call to be humble to a select group of Christians. There is great respect for those dedicating their lives to prayer, meditation, and work with little or no salary. Our assumption seems one of thinking, "Well, after they have spent long hours devoted in solitude to God, they can come into the public view upon occasion and live the kind of the life our Lord says we are to live." They are our representatives in this whole business of humility. Praise God, He made that style of living for some — very few in my opinion — but you and I dare not lean on them for our own salvation!

Why is it we seem to think it is only possible to serve God to the fullest extent separate, apart, and isolated from society? We are not to discount those who do, but the great masses of mankind are not created for such a life. Aren't we afraid of being too different and suffering the consequences a world — not knowing Christ — will superimpose upon us? Again it's a matter of thinking through a partial truth. It isn t that the cloistered life is bad. Quite the contrary is true for the few. It is the entrapment tactic of the devil which points out that since there are those who can evidence Christ's call to be humble from time to time we are excluded. It is as though they are an official appeasement to an expectant God, a kind of burnt offering to compensate for our failure.

I like the First Century Church's understanding of sainthood. Saints were all Christians or "holy ones."

Paul says in Romans 1:7, "To all God's beloved in Rome, who are called to be saints . . ." Can we expect in our time for the call to be humble to be anything less than it was in New Testament times?

Now, we are ready for our final point.

"It is workable here and now for all professing His name" is the fourth reaction.

This, too, is an honest reaction. I'm sure in our Lord's prayers, especially those upon the Cross, He sought for future followers to react in this way. It gives credibility to His message. It moves Him out of the purely ideal and into the realm of behavior that can actually take place. He was the lowly Galilean and our excuses and even fights over the right policy or architecture of churches He must find a questionable appendage to His word for us. While we cannot deny the necessity of civilization and the importance of culture, we ought to be hungry and thirsty after this fourth reaction in the lives of people.

What do we have to give up in order for this to become a reality in daily situations? "Who knows" is as good an answer as any. We do not really know until we come before His throne every day with the admission that such a life is workable for those professing Jesus the Christ as Savior and Lord. So many of us like the idea of His being Savior, but to be Lord . . . well, that's a bit more than we want. However, to proclaim Him is to move beyond the conversion experience and make of us practicing Christians who take Churchmanship seriously. Saint Paul's little prepositional phrase "in Christ" tells us, among many other things, that for the Christian to move into a serious and joyous encounter with the Bible is to put our lives in a different dimension from a system of negatives or "What do we have to give up?" stance. We are to deal in spiritual additions and multiplications, not subtractions and divisions.

Sometimes single, one-syllable words make all the difference in upward mobility in the religious experience. In this instance I am referring to the little ones "to" and "for." To come to terms with our Lord's call to be humble is not met by "What's it going to do 'to' us?" The proper question, of course, is "What is it going to do 'for' us?" There is a tendency, powerful and in a sense demonic, that can see only how we will be degraded, deformed, and defamed by what the living out of our Lord's call will do "to" us. He pleads with you and me to see what it will do "for" us. After all, praise God, we are not dealing with an obscure passage out of the Old Testament. We are in the presence of the living Word brought to us by the Christ! Indeed, has it ever occurred to us the beggar may not need our handout at all? We may need to give it to him in order to become what Christ calls us to be.

IV.

From the very beginning you and I were and are called to be humble.

The Sermon on the Mount relays to us this special message: "You have heard that it was said, 'An eye for an eye, and a tooth for a tooth.' But I say to you, Do not resist one who is evil. But if anyone strikes you on the right cheek, turn to him the other also; and if any one would sue you and take your coat, let him have your cloak as well; and if anyone forces you to go one mile, go with him two miles. Give to him who begs from you, and do not refuse him who would borrow from you."

Our honest reactions are in a foursome: this isn't workable; it may be workable, but it will make us into jellyfishes; it it workable for only those willing to live a cloistered life; and it is workable here and now for all professing His name.

To be called to be humble by the Christ is to have the strength through Him to attain the goal.

CALLED TO BE RESILIENT
Matthew 5:43-45

I.

"Hang loose" and "Be able to bend or you will break" are timely pieces of advice.

They say Christians must be resilient or able to respond affirmatively to all situations in the highest and best sense. The world would tell us there is an element of compromise in life that would necessitate our "giving in' at some important points. Of course, that is not in keeping with the "highest and best." The world has a way of twisting and turning our Faith into the expedient, not the excellent. You and I are bought with a price, namely the sacrifice of Jesus upon the Cross, and we must not allow the world to intervene and weaken. The truth in homey jewels of wisdom is invariably open to a reduction in spiritual insight. It would seem there are those who have mistaken such common sense approaches for the real thing which is the blessed gift of Christ to us in the form of right living. So there is often a delicate balance between the person who knows how to apply a gentle but manipulative humanism and the one who is a Christian seeking to grow in the Faith.

Admittedly, it is a day when schedules, modes of thinking, etc., can be changed at the twinkling of an eye. Unless we can make some sort of reasonable adjustment to these integral parts of our lives, we had best find a cave . . . of course, it might be subject to being covered by a new reservoir or blasted away to make room for a new industry. Christians are copers, that is, they can take such things in stride, not because of their brilliant techniques but because their Lord overcame the world. Our Faith is not dependent on geographic location or just the right set of circumstances. Our Lord comes to terms with both and yet is above both. Otherwise, our Faith would be severely limited and perhaps made into just another mediocre attempt to deal with the precariousness of human existence.

Our Blessed Lord points the way to a victorious life unfragmented and not cursed by the keeping of "love-hate" records.

In Matthew 5:43-45 a clear course is set before us: "You have heard that it was said, 'You shall love your neighbor and hate your enemy.' But I say to you, Love your enemies and pray for those who persecute you, so that you may be sons of your Father who is in heaven; for he makes his sun rise on the evil and on the good, and sends rain on the just and on the unjust." These are not easy words to implement. This is often true of Jesus, isn't it? Yet, He does not open the way to do something and then tell us it isn't possible.

These few words showed a pagan world what it was not and His Jewish brethren what they could be.

II.

You and I are called to be resilient.

We all like to see where a decisive decision leads us.

Just where does our Lord's call take us?

III.

It resists the temptation "to right wrongs."

"An eye for an eye and a tooth for a tooth" was an improved way of dealing with wrongs long ago, but it is not the final and lofty revelation given to us by the Christ. Our Lord caringly nudges us to move beyond a mere calculation of justice. His way brings love into the dynamics of human relations. It does not seek an equal hurt for an equal hurt. When we stop to ponder, that sort of system leads no place beyond a strict keeping of records in the real and/or imagined injuries of life. That within itself is enough to keep our minds focused on judgment. Saint Paul says in Philippians 4:8, "Finally, brethren, whatever is true, whatever is honorable, whatever is just, whatever is pure, whatever is lovely, whatever is gracious, if there is any excellence, if there is anything worthy of praise, think about these things." Notice that while the word "just" is mentioned, it is among the true, honorable, pure, lovely, and gracious. Lincoln caught the vision of the Christ's message in his Second Inaugural Address: "With malice toward none; with charity for all; with firmness in the right as God gives us to see the right ..."

Perhaps the most detrimental spirit is that which applies a keen eye into making everything come out even in life. To be sure that is an improvement over anarchy. Yet, it has so many loopholes because I cannot walk in your shoes and you cannot walk in mine. Our Lord maintains victorious living — yes, right living — cannot be found in keeping score. Some seem to have a filing cabinet overflowing with folders listing and categorizing wrongs. Then upon what they consider suitable occasions they drag out their dregs in an attempt to drive home a point. Christ must shed a tear when He sees this happening. It is so opposed to His Sermon on the Mount, especially the test before us.

Our call entails a resiliency which enables us to bounce back at a person who has wronged us and say, "I love you." This is what Christ's life was all about. It is what ours — within the Faith — is all about. When we are stripped and beaten figuratively or literallly, we are to love and pray for those committing such acts. The spirit of Christ in each of us always has the power to spring back, not in hurtful retaliation, but in loving consideration of the gospel message.

Where does the call to be resilient take us next?

It resolves to move beyond the mere keeping of a set of rules.

Many writers and seemingly much of the media make light of our time having few moral standards and keeping even fewer. While this appears to keep us in a twilight zone morally, I am not sure it is all bad. Sterility in the religious life is often marked by spending a lot of time deciding into which column particular actions and thoughts belong. From time to time we may need to do some analyzing. However, as a style of living we can approach the dangerous levels attained by some whose self-righteousness is a contradiction of our Lord's life and message. It is possible to be the epitome of a highly respected morality and know nothing of the saving grace of God through Christ. You might argue that this state of affairs is rare, but I am not so sure that it is. A person has to acknowledge his or her sins before repentance can take place. Saint Paul tells us in Romans 3:23 "since all have sinned and fall short of the glory of God." That doesn't leave much room for exacting regulations — regardless of how noble they appear to be — separate and apart from the conversion experience through Christ, does it?

Our Lord's way is away from rigidity and toward a saving resiliency. He doesn't say, "Now, here is your neighbor; love him. Over there is your enemy; hate him." To utilize a common phrase today "he puts it all together." Well, doesn't He? Some might even go so far as to say, "Jesus had His head on straight." Our Lord was in touch with the depths of human nature, even that part which appears to intend the very best. He knew there were many who if given a favorable environment would and could exercise the will power to be moral giants. He also knew that created a situation which led to only one conclusion: righteousness before God, self-achieved. We are reminded of His word to us in Matthew 23:13: "But woe to you, scribes and Pharisees, hypocrites! because you shut the kingdom of heaven against men; for you neither enter yourselves, nor allow those who would enter to go in."

So, our Lord's teaching is in a real sense a resolve to keep changing man from the inside out with an on going, evident marriage of faith and works.

Where else does the call to be resilient take us?

It respects the new dimensions Christ brought to the Judeo-Christian Faith.

Often Jesus begins with "You have heard it said ..." He is updating His followers. He brings them something better. The old ways don't allow for the right priority; the right one is, of course, to love in all situations. While Jesus has been depicted as a revolutionist by many, in reality He was probably an evolutionist. His teaching stretches that already in existence and thereby brings to His people, the Jews, a new and dynamic way of looking at life.

Today as Christian members of the Church it takes you and me into those blessed but sometimes very unsettling heights. What if we love our enemies and pray for our persecutors ... then they turn on us with renewed hostility and kill or mutilate us? Our first reaction may be, "Well, that just isn't the way it is supposed to work." To react that way is to second-guess what our Lord has in mind. My, how we do get in the way of the Faith revealed to us! Lest we forget, the latter part of the text reads: "for he makes his sun rise on the evil and on the good, and sends rain on the just and on the unjust." You and I are not a favored people — "a royal priesthood" — because we are exempt from God's overall and everlasting purposes. We are favored because we have seen the light of Calvary and accepted His Son, regardless of where we are led. The blood of martyrs is always a part of the landscape as we survey our Faith. You and I may need to have our memories refreshed that we are in truth also parts of that landscape. Even while the clergy read accounts of the Church through the ages and are thrilled by the sacrifices of those gone before, they are summoned to the altar of accountability for they too are now in their own lives writing Church history.

There is a tendency after the exhilaration of the converson experience of commitment to Christ has dimmed for us to nestle down into pathways most conducive to our comfort. Indeed, we might even skip over our text. God forgive us! The Crown is never ours without the Cross. I fear some will attempt to claim a crown, tainted by the refusal to be responsive and responsible to this portion of the Sermon on the Mount.

In 1887 for his graduating class at Andover Theological Seminary, Ernest Warburton Shurtleff wrote:

Lead on, O King Eternal,
We follow, not with fears,
For gladness breaks like morning
Where'ere thy face appears.
Thy Cross is lifted o'er us;
We journey in its light;
The Crown awaits the conquest;
Lead on, O God of might.

Finally, where does the call to be resilient take us?

It restores a basic integrity necessary for us to be authentic witnesses.

Mainline denominations have been hit often and hard by the modern proverb "We are just like everyone else trying to serve man and reach the same destination." While such a saw may have been essential for a time to keep our feet on the ground and in touch with humanity, it has now, in my opinion, neared the end of its usefulness. Christians are not "just like everyone else." They are a special people — "called out" — who do not set out to lord it over others because of their superior way of life. They (you and me, if you please) call upon their Lord to lead them that they may be known for their authenticity before their brothers and sisters, some within and some outside of the Fold. The great theologian Soren Kierkegaard attacked the Church of his day in a sense because everyone was like everyone else, members of the Church for the most part, but unwilling to come to terms with the Word which called for undivided loyalty to Christ.

A well-known Episcopal layman, William Stringfellow, says in his book **Conscience and Obedience:** "A most obstinate misconception associated with the gospel of Jesus Christ is that the gospel is welcome in the world." That is prophetic! Christian laity and clergy alike should listen and give thanks someone has the courage not only to say it but put it into print. Our call to resiliency is not one that promises attractiveness, popularity, success, or even progress as the world understands those inviting, nice terms. Saint Paul comes on strong in Ephesians 6:14 when he says, "Stand therefore, having girded your loins with truth, and having put on the breastplate of righteousness." That does not in any way, shape, or form lay before us the requirement to get lost in a crowd of pilgrims pushing and shoving us towards goals of peace and goodwill given definition and made sacred by a very surface kind of Faith, hardly worthy of the name.

Our voyage is nearly complete for now.

IV.

Christians are called to be resilient.

52

Listen again to the glorious and always pertinent word from our Blessed Lord: "You have heard that it was said, 'You shall love your neighbor and hate your enemy.' But I say to you, Love your enemies and pray for those who persecute you, so that you may be sons of your Father who is in heaven; for he makes his sun rise on the evil and on the good, and sends rain on the just and on the unjust."

To decide decisively on the call for our lives lays before us not the routine "three r's" but the majestic appeal of four which contain a built-in selling quality for those genuinely seeking a closer walk with the Christ: **resisting** the temptation "to right wrongs;" **resolving** to move beyond the mere keeping of a set of rules; **respecting** the new dimensions Christ brought to the Judeo-Christian Faith; and **restoring** a basic integrity necessary for us to be authentic witnesses.

The serious (and joyous) followers of the Christ cope with today's living by hearing and obeying the call to be resilient.

CALLED TO BE LOW-PROFILE
Matthew 6:1

I.

What can be done for Christ and the Church that will definitely be seen?

What are your reactions to such a question? If they are like mine, they are mixed. In fact they run the gamut from a radical selfishness to an extreme unselfishness. What can be any more selfish than an attempt to seek the honor and adulation of people by insisting that a gift or service be accompanied by all the fanfare a public relations man can conjure up? On the other hand, what can be any more selfless than an attempt to do something really sacrificial and beneficial for our Lord and His Body, the Church? It's so amazing what we can see or not see as we look at an attempt to be seen for our piety.

I am reminded of the two shoe salesmen who were told by their company to seek a new market in Africa. One saw hundreds and thousands of natives without shoes. His conclusion: We might as well forget about this place because there is no chance of selling our shoes here. The other saw the same hundreds and thousands shoeless. His conclusion: There is great opportunity here because no one has sold them any.

Our initial question is a "sticky wicket," isn't it? Who can know why a person(s) does what he or she does? That is perhaps the most intriguing probe we can set out to do on anyone. We enter into the personhood of individuals at the point where crucial and decisive decisions are made. We feel as though we have come into that sacred ground defined as the soul. "Destiny" is staring at us with a person's relationship to God being observed as it is. Are we beginning to "play god?" Perhaps. At any rate, I invite you to move to a spiritual imperative.

Jesus the Christ places before us a text that makes us come to grips with motives.

Matthew 6:1 is a solemn warning: "Beware of practicing your piety before men in order to be seen by them; for then you will have no reward from your Father who is in heaven." Like so much of the Sermon on the Mount, this is a verse we would just as soon bypass. It calls for more tha an activist Faith. It causes us sometimes to look inward and cry out, "Lord, why did I do that?"

We take the call to be low-profile lightly at our own risk. The Apostles learned that. You and I should also.

II.

Our Lord leaves no doubt as to our being called to be low-profile.

Let's move to the heart of the matter and pose the question that has to be addressed sooner or later.

What motivates persons to practice their religion in order to be seen?

III.

The desire to perpetuate their memory is certainly one.

Well, what is wrong with that? Surely no one can find fault in wanting to be remembered as a religious person. There are many today saying we just don't have enough of that kind of thing. How do we even begin to mount an argument against such a noble idea? Why should we? Isn't it self-evident that this is a right motive? I would like to be known as a good person in the year 2100, wouldn't you? The thought of my descendants saying "He was a good man" makes my eyes water in hope it will happen. It seems to me there is some of this in everyone professing the Christian Faith.

However, our Lord's point is deeply personal and we have to deal with it. To pray aloud in the market place to be seen by others who would marvel at such a display apparently was rather common in our Lord's day. The meaning of the text is clear: to do such a thing is to make impossible a reward in heaven. Another illustration, common to that day and time, was fasting in such a way that everybody within seeing and hearing distance knew you were giving up food and paying a high price for doing so. This was cause for men to extend the highest of praises to those taking their religion seriously. There seems to have been a strain of sophisticated wickedness which called attention to an open and noisy practice of religion that was little more than a reasonable good acting job before others.

To be religious with trumpets blowing, sirens sounding, and spotlights beaming to perpetuate one's quality of the religious life is just not the way we are to practice our piety. While our day is gifted with media that can bring to us the finest and best in religious programming, one cannot help wondering about the eventual impact of some shows. Is the gospel of our Lord and Savior, Jesus the Christ, being spread or are we falling victim to a "show biz" that impudently claims the blessing of God without consulting God? Alongside every great opportunity for good there seems to be a corresponding one for bad. The Faith must be practiced or lived in order to be legitimate. However, to seek the acclaim of future generations is to cancel out any eternal reward.

What is the next motive that would do away with our call to be low-profile?

The desire to "lay up treasures in heaven" is one.

We are all aware of the temptation to bargain with God. Sometimes this degenerates into not only a crass exercise but a satanic curse. The layout is basically the same, isn't it? "God, if You will reserve that mansion with the swimming pool and tennis court, I will begin tithing from my gross income by check." "God, if You will place a permanent lease on the condominium on the same floor as so and so, I will read my Bible every day and fast once each week in public." Farfetched, unrealistic, and irrelevant? Knowing what I know about the deepest recesses of some hearts, I really don't think so. There are those who appear to have the audacity to believe that even God can be conned.

I have known some fine people and so have you who have assumed the more expressive they were in their religious lives the greater the quality of their religion. Somehow to shout, sing loudly, cry profusely, and shake hands almost with a vengeance indicated there was a laying up of treasure in heaven. The style seemed to be one of "the more we can show how much we love Jesus the more His followers will see us and the more jewels we will have in our crown." Pershaps you and I are not expressive enough and this reflects an inner famine. We don't want to be seen of men at all because we don't have anything to show them. If that be the case, may God fill us to the brim and overflowing with the riches found in His Son. Sometimes members of mainline denominations are caught in the quandary of either proclaiming a very vocal — even ostentatious — type of religion or pussy-footing along with a timid variety that doesn't really have much worthwhile to say because it knows so very little about the Man of Galilee. The fruit of the spirit, according to Galatians 5:22-23, "is love, joy, peace, patience, kindness, goodness, faithfulness, gentleness, self-control . . ." Those words have a way of resolving the problems with which we are dealing, don't they?

Awaiting us is another avenue bringing insight on the matter.

The desire to impress their fellows is a powerful motivation.

The words from the Epistle of James are appropriate: "For where jealousy and selfish ambition exist, there will be disorder and every vile practice" (3:16). Clergy and laity find common problems here. It makes no difference what policy is operating or particular beliefs are emphasized. There are those who will do anything to get their way and this often involves a display of piety. This is as old as the church. James was speaking out of the First Century.

Those who say they do not believe in a devil should know some of the internal workings of any body or group that bears the name of a religious organization. The finest disciplines of the Christian life can be perverted to the point of being nothing more than tools to elevate someone into a position of power and prominence. Such odious games are more than merely offensive and detrimental; they are tragic, death-dealing blemishes on the very Body of Christ. In Luke 13:34 Jesus laments: "O Jerusalem, Jerusalem killing the prophets and stoning those who are sent to you! How often would I have gathered your children together as a hen gathers her brood under her wings and you would not!"

We smile at the person who looks at another and says, "I can out-humble you." Yet, this is a manner in which some seem to deal with their planned rise to stardom. Such an attitude finds its way to all levels where men, women, youth, and children come together. Some wag has said with scorching pertinence: "That man prays his best and gives generously to the poor as the cameras click away."

One more motive comes into our midst.

The desire to outdo others manages to simmer away.

Saint Paul was a remarkably competitive man, but there is no place in his epistles advocating the display of piety for the purpose of being seen. He bubbled over with enthusiasm for the Faith. Many caught his divine disease. Any time he was attempting to outdo others it was with a twinkle in his eye urging them to run with him. One gets the feeling there is a boyish sincerity in his love for the Faith which has the effect of making competitors out of those whose religion was either out-and-out pagan or rotten and ineffectual from stagnation.

The serious athlete in every sport wants to win. That's only natural. The serious Christian wants to win in the skirmishes of life. That's only natural. Some well-known professional was heard to say, "Winning isn't everything; it's the only thing." In a sense that's true for the Christian. However, our winning formula is found in summary form in John's Gospel: "Jesus said to him, 'I am the way and the truth, and the life; no one comes to the Father, but by me!" (14:6). It is through the lowly Galilean the race is run and hopefully won; that gives us just the right perspectives and dimensions for victorious living in the Faith without drawing adulatory attention to ourselves.

With typical Pauline understanding we conclude our final part: "Let love be genuine; hate what is evil, hold fast to what is good; love one another with brotherly affection; outdo one another in showing honor. Never flag in zeal, be aglow with the Spirit, serve the Lord." (Romans 12:9-11)

IV.

Yes, you and I — professing Christians — are called to be low-profile.

Our Lord doesn't waste a single word as He bids us with a firm hand: "Beware of practicing your piety before men in order to be seen by them; for then you will have no reward from your Father who is in heaven."

We can see within others (and especially ourselves), at least, some of the motivations to forsake this call: the desire to perpetuate their (our)memory, to "lay up treasures in heaven." to impress their (our) fellows, to be prominent in the Church, and to outdo others.

You and I hear the call, don't we? It provides the surest and most complete way for our light to shine. Ah, let us sing a song of victory and hope as we "trust and obey for there is no other way to be happy in Jesus!"

CALLED TO BE SECLUSIVE
Matthew 6:5-6

I.

The most awesome of all privileges is to be alone with God.

Think of it! A conversation with the Almighty can and does happen. We — you and I — speak and He listens. Then aren't we blessed beyond words as the reverse happens! Finity meets Infinity and the heavens shake! While it is a privileged experience, it is also an escape hatch. Self is always limited and sometimes, let's face it, we have no other place to go except to God. During the Civil War (War Between the States) Lincoln was heard to say, "I was driven to my knees because I had no place else to go." The eternal God of the universe bends low and hears our whimpers, joys, sorrows, and disilusionments. James Weldon Johnson in "The Creation" catches the mood so well when he says:

> This great God,
> Like a mammy bending over her baby,
> Kneeled down in the dust
> Toiling over a lump of clay
> Till he shaped it in his own image;
> Then into it he blew the breath of life,
> And man became a living soul.
> Amen. Amen.

Some may be pondering in reaction, "All well and good. Now just where does Jesus fit into all of this?" He is the Christ. As perfectly God and man He brings to us the peak revelation of the caring God most clearly expressed by His love. For you and I to be able to visit with God in the way we do is because of His son, Jesus. From one vantage point, ours is a double and even triple privilege. To know God in three persons — Father, Son, and Holy Spirit — ministers to the toal religious life as does no other persuasion. The twin events of the Crucifixion and Resurrection sealed with perfection the most complete way to know God. It is not that He was absent in the lives and histories of peoples before our Lord's birth. It is that He chose not to reveal Himself fully until the physical presence of His Son upon this planet.

The Christ lays out before us a specific, elevating the intimacy of our Faith.

In Matthew 6:5-6 He gives us a profound pointer on prayer: "And when you pray, you must not be like the hypocrites; for they love to stand and pray in the synagogues and at the street corners that they may be seen by men. Truly, I say to you, they have their reward. But when you pray, go into your room and shut the door and pray to your Father who is in secret; and your Father who sees in secret will reward you." Two comments are helpful. One is that this is not the only word about prayer in the New Testament given to us by Him. The other is we dare not say this is the only proper way to pray.

II.

To gain the most edification from our topic we are wise to narrow and sharpen it. An inquiry does this. What are the advantages in the call to be seclusive in our prayer lives?

III.

In the first place there is the direct one-on-one relationship with God.

For many — probably most — This is a religious experience that goes unequaled. It is the survival tactic surpassing all others. To go to God in prayer with the world's problems and sins beating upon us is not optional ... that is, if we are to continue sane. To be able to fall on our knees in seclusion with God often literally saves the day ... and some lives. Our entire existence as Christians is ruptured without it. We are meant to be in tune with our Father and sometimes in the privacy of our own rooms. Aren't we pleasantly surprised to learn such rooms do not have to bear our legal ownership? We may find ourselves in a hotel or motel many miles from our residences and be blessed by our Lord's instruction. I have known those who could receive solace no other way. Even the churches were not private enough. In fact, many of our churches in large cities are locked, except on Sunday morning. Would you believe there are those during the week who have ministers, secretaries, and others busily working away who are shut off from the outside by locks? Why? Largely because of the known pilferage, destruction, and outright desecration that has taken place when doors were left open. Our Lord's Word begins to have even more relevance, doesn't it?

We miss an opportunity unless we personalize. Don't we all remember instances of closed sessions with our Lord? It may have been a matter of having our feelings deeply hurt. Someone may not have appreciated your hard, volunteer work in the Church and even severely criticized it before others. It's difficult to deal with those things, isn't it? Yet, God has very big shoulders upon which to cry. Whether we moan, groan, or attempt to atone for our heinous sins, He is present. Do you ever cry with joy and happiness in this blessed one-on-one relationship? I think most of us have had that experience. There is nothing quite like it, is there? A teenager said recently, "I love to pray to God alone, knowing I can just let it all hang out." I suspect there are any number of adults, perhaps fathers and mothers or even grandparents, who wish they could feel the closeness of God behind closed doors that they felt as teens. It is so very important not only to receive our Lord early in life but to keep growing in the Faith. To do so means the presence of God becomes more real and not less so.

You and I take for granted that we can pray to God in our private sanctuaries and be heard. There is great assurance and security in this. Really could we go on living without it? I don't think so. I happen to think that when a person stops talking to God, he or she either has or will suffer spiritual death. The provision has been made for us to go directly to Him, hasn't it? It is life-giving. If for no other reason, it keeps man aware that he never exists apart from the God who made him. More specifically, as Christians we share in the blessings bought for us by the sacrificial death of Christ. The most dreaded of all pictures is that of the human being who cannot go to his or her God because God refuses to allow it. Talk about having one's spiritual heart ripped out! That, if it became a reality, would do it.

In our own small but sincere way let's thank God for the privilege of coming to Him as Jesus says "in secret." Our hearts should sing with joy. Our minds should phrase and rephrase poems of gratitude.

What is another advantage in the call to be seclusive in our prayer lives?

In the second place there is the privacy of "telling all."

For most — perhaps all — Christians it is only in such an environment that all sins can be brough out into the open. In Galatians 5:19-21 Saint Paul spells out the works of the flesh: "immorality, impurity, licentiousness, idolatry, sorcery, enmity, strife, jealousy, anger, selfishness, dissension, party spirit, envy, drunkenness, carousing, and the like." This listing of "dirty linen" that injures far more than those directly afflicted can, for most of us, be brought into the open only in our private sanctuaries. The purging process is rightly between God and man. Praise His Name, there is that intermediary, Jesus the Christ, whose saving powers fall upon us like heavenly sunshine. We should not underestimate the assistance and concern of other Christian pilgrims. At the same time we must not overestimate them. Each is personally accountable before God.

Life that is worth living can continue only as we unload before Him who created us and gave to us His Blessed Son. Repentance is a word some theologians, and apparently quite a number of laypersons, have attempted to strike from their vocabularies. Of course, this is not possible . . . that is, if one seeks the mercies of God. We are all sinners saved by the grace of God through His Son. While we may tend to blame evil forces at work in our environment that contaminate us, man is a sinner from the time of birth. The glorious message from our Lord is that we do not have to be lost and eventually claimed by hell, or whatever name we choose to designate the place where those who deliberately refuse the Savior are sent.

The sweetest and most all-pervasive, splendid word in the English language is ''forgiven.'' How many times have you and I laid our souls bare before God and been disappointed? Oh, we may need to plead and know anguish first-hand. Yet, I doubt that anyone who really repents has forgiveness withheld. Our God is faithful, just, and merciful. Kate Hankey, an enthusiastic Angelican Sunday School teacher, says in brief simplicity what you and I know as forgiveness is granted:

> I love to tell the story,
> 'Twill be my theme in glory,
> To tell the old, old story
> Of Jesus and his love.

Sometimes we Christians forget that God is forgetful. Does that sound irreverent? If it does, just consider one statement: "If we confess our sins, he is faithful and just, and will forgive our sins and cleanse us from all unrighteousness." (1 John 1:9) You and I may not be fully able to escape the consequences of our sins, but that does not mean God's forgiveness comes with strings attached. To be forgiven is to be forgiven. Of course, it is apropos to jog our memories about what Jesus said to the woman caught in adultery: ".. go, and do not sin again." (John 8:11)

We now turn to a final advantage in the call to be seclusive in our prayer lives.

In the third place, there is the freedom of asking for what we really want.

It's a "no holds barred atmosphere," isn't it? Just as soon as the recognition comes to us that a single soul and God are alone, the reality of petitioning for what we deeply want is transparent. There is a trust at work that moves out of the range of vocabularies. That enigmatic but spectacular Book of Revelation provides us with a timely and timeless image: "Behold, I stand at the door and knock; if anyone hears my voice and opens the door, I will come in to him and eat with him, and he with me." (3:20) To dine with Christ captures the spirit of God and man's greatest love affair. Our Lord sits across the table from us and with barriers down we can look into His face and speak with confidence. What our Faith has hopefully taught the other religions of the world is that God through Christ is approachable. He is so approachable, in fact, that we can share the same table, food, and drink. That's an internationally significant banquet for two!

The thought may have occurred to you as it has to me, "What if I ask for the wrong thing?" My reaction is scriptural: "But if God so clothes the grass which is alive in the field today and tomorrow is thrown into the oven, how much more will he clothe you, O men of little faith!" (Luke 12:28) Isn't it exciting to be able to experience the depths in conversations with God! Is this questionable mysticism? I do not see how it can be in view of the promises made in the Bible. You and I repeatedly claim too little for our Faith. The tune of R. Kelso Carter's hymn draws us to it, but what about the words? That very reassuring second stanza powerfully oozes with a victorious spirit:

> Standing on the promises that cannot fail,
> When the howling storms of doubt and fear
>   assail
> By the living Word of God I shall prevail,
> Standing on the promises of God.*

There is great joy in being relieved of all defenses and simply requesting from our Lord and Savior that for which we cry out.

IV.

We are called to be seclusive in our prayer lives.

Let us hear again those words of instruction from the master Teacher: "And when you pray, you must not be like the hypocrites; for they love to stand and pray in the synagogues and at the street corners, that they may be seen by men. Truly, I say to you, they have their reward. But when you pray, go into your room and shut the door and pray to your Father who is in secret; and your Father who sees in secret will reward you."

The advantages to such a call are momentous and bear the marks of spiritual destiny: there is the direct one-on-one relationship with God; the privacy of "telling all;" and the freedom of asking for what we really want.

If we have not already done so, it is past time to decide to meet God in seclusion — at least — once each day ... unhurriedly.

CALLED TO BE CONCISE
Matthew 6:7-8

I.

There is real art in saying important things in a few words.

A number of years ago a New York City newspaper reported: "The creation of the world is told in Genesis in 400 words. The Ten Commandments have only 297 words, and the Declaration of Independence has 1,821 words, but a government pamphlet required 2,500 words to announce a reduction in the price of cabbage seed." This illustration remains typical of the way lives are lived and institutions operated today. It seems a basic decision was made a number of years ago — and no one noticed — to major in minors or to spend long hours and money in producing countless words to say less and less. One observer has noted with a cynical twist, "Our day will go down in history as one chiefly characterized by verbal and written diarrhea."

From a more positive standpoint, we have to confront the information explosion. How and why have we come to this time in our civilization: Largely through the brilliance, dedication, and energy of men and women is the obvious answer. The sciences and social sciences have entered worlds that fifty years ago our progenitors only dreamed about, and then with considerable vagueness. We have blessings piled on top of blessings in the struggle to bring quality to our lives. I can't recall of talking to anyone ready to turn the clock back a hundred or even fifty years. However, just as we finish saying this, we see picture after picture of looters who took advantage of a technological failure.

68

Where does all of this lead? Hopefully, it should lead us back on our knees to a serious probing of the Bible. If that is being reactionary, then I plead guilty.

The Master drives to the heart of the problem for those caught up in too many words in an attempt to be religious.

It doesn't take Him long to cut through the peelings of some sour and rotting apples, as He says in Matthew 6:7-8: "And in praying do not heap up empty phrases as the Gentiles do; for they think that they will be heard for their many words. Do not be like them, for your Father knows what you need before you ask him." That contains forty-one words. If you are in a hurry, they can be said audibly in ten seconds.

You and I are called to be concise. There is, at least, one special meaning in this call. It warrants our undeserved attention.

II.

Called to be concise means especially putting together what we expect from our God. While He knows before we ask, it is for us to know what we are asking.

Saint Paul's desire in 1 Corinthians 14:19 assists in moving to these expectations: ". . . I would rather speak five words with my mind, in order to instruct others, than ten thousand words in a tongue." It seems to me as professing Christians all expectations from God fall under just five headings.

III.

We expect God to control by a loving captivity.

The plea of countless souls through the centuries has been, "Oh, loving God, don't let loose of me!" Better than anyone else the Christian knows the meaning of dependency. This comes about not because of a belittling of self but because of the recognition and acceptance of the absolute greatness of God. Jonathan Edwards captured this sense of awesomeness in his sermon known throughout the world, "Sinners in the Hands of an Angry God." He says to the unconverted: "There is nothing between you and hell but the air; 'tis only the power and mere pleasure of God that holds you up." The Christian knows he or she is held captive by a loving God and that this relationship was brought about by Jesus the Christ, both Savior and Lord. Isn't it miraculous the way in which our pleas are answered? Sometimes we have "thrown in the towel" and as a last bit of desperation have pleaded with God, who we discover has been holding us securely with tender loving care in His hand all along.

The saints have understood for centuries that freedom is found in loving captivity. It is not exaggeration to maintain this is a basic reason for their sainthood. You and I can proclaim to the world as did the Apostle Paul, ". . . for when I am weak, then I am strong." (2 Corinthians 12:10) That proclamation, typical of all who seriously profess His name, is really given birth by the Son's prayer to the Father: ". . . Nevertheless not my will, but thine, be done." (Luke 22:42) Then a short time later we read that Jesus was allowed to experience the horror of God's forsaking Him, which is a precious prelude to the Resurrection showing God had not let loose of Him at all. That's the kind of religion we have. Let's rejoice in it! We turn to a second central item.

We expect God to bestow righteous equity.

Deep down everyone knows total equality and justice can come only from God. For one thing, you and I are unable to see beyond this brief stay. This isn't our fault. God made us that way. In the final sense, God is the Chief Universal Executive who administers all of His creation. You and I have a right to expect Him to deal with every human being on an impartial basis. Saint Peter, in Acts 10:34, tells us, "Truly I perceive that God shows no partiality." Saint Paul, in Romans 2:11, speaks: "For God shows no partiality." God is eternally wise and in time treats everyone alike. That's hard for us to accept at times because our own wisdom and our sense of being impartial are clouding the picture.

If you have lived very many years at all, you have felt like shouting, "That's unfair!" I have seen situations and you have in which, by every measurement, the person was treated unfairly. Even to stretch the imagination, there seemed to be a gross lack of justice. There is only One who can straighten out our thinking. His name is Jesus the Christ, who must have been the world's most ill-treated person in the closing weeks of His life. What had Jesus done wrong ... except bring truth into their midst? Of course, "the truth hurts" is a cliche that deserves our attention now and then. Saint Paul's life was plagued by hurts, hates, and hostilities; yet, he sketches for Christians a landscape giving us a glorious glimpse of the way God chooses to relate to us. In the way of love he says, "For now we see in a mirror dimly, but then face to face. Now I know in part; then I shall understand fully, even as I have been fully understood." (1 Corinthians 13:12)

What is our third expectation?

We expect God to provide spiritual prosperity.

This is a simple statement of what the New Testament proclaims on page after page. The good news is the gospel and vice versa. The Pauline Epistles are the working out of the gospel in the lives of precious persons in specific geographic areas. Luke shows, in the Acts of the Apostles, the Church moving mightily forward. The general or catholic epistles speak to Christians wherever they are. The Revelation to John tells us of the end of an age. The statement that best summarizes our present expectation is that found in the Gospel of John: "... I came that they may have life, and have it abundantly." (10:10) Granted, adversity may abound and it is difficult — if not well-nigh impossible for a time — to discover the truth in our Lord's words. Nevertheless, the saints have shown us repeatedly that spiritual prosperity may only become a reality in some of the most unpromising situations.

As usual, you and I get foggy about the difference between His concept of being prosperous and ours. Many of today's most popular speakers and writers don't help much. There's a partial — even veneer — witness to the truth which puts bandaids on ravaging malignancies. We are reminded of that miraculous drug, hadacol, of several years ago. When it was found to have a high content of alcohol and little else, it was no longer considered to be a wonder-worker for humanity. God's storehouse is always dispensing blessing to and for us. It is our lack of depth in the ways of the Master that causes us to belittle or disown them. Saint Paul instructs us to "give thanks in all circumstances; for this is the will of God in Christ Jesus for you." (1 Thessalonians 5:18)

In our call to be concise we now move to the fourth heading.

We expect God to look after posterity.

Our forefathers were especially keen on this matter. Much of their drive in felling trees, building homes, combatting diseases, and working sixteen hours a day was directly connected to making the world a better place for those who would follow. The greatness of our nation in terms of human wisdom owes a debt it cannot repay to those who died from overexertion and battling the hardships of an untamed America. Today many of the same thoughts of building a better world for those who follow must be uppermost in the minds of people in Brazil, Canada, and Australia. While we may want to romanticize those who paved the way for us, it was a common belief that God was and would be responsible for the better life coming with each generation. Our nation is still young in comparison to England, France, Spain, and many others that go back centuries. Nevertheless, our ties to those in the 17th, 18th, and 19th centuries carving out a nation are strong and we should look upon them in loving gratitude.

You and I look to God to provide for those who are following and will follow us. I want those who follow me to know God through Jesus the Christ, don't you? Our prayers do not go amiss as we offer them on behalf of those who are yet unborn. It is never enough for the Christian father and mother to know they are safely in the Fold. They want some assurances their children and grandchildren also will know and serve Christ the Savior and Lord. One of the most inspiring and stirring sentences I have read recently was in **Rediscovering Prayer** by John L. Casteel: "Some person will recall how the habit of prayer shaped the spirit of family ancestors, and will recognize that though they themselves do not pray, they are what they are in no small degree because their grandparents did." Some of the basics of the Faith, including our prayer lives, have been on the verge of extinction in recent years. We owe it to those in the year 2000 and beyond to pray often in sincerity and humility. Then, we can rightfully expect God to care for them.

Finally, what do we expect of Him who rules the universe?

We expect God to grant material necessity.

There are elementary needs for living a good life. I, for one, believe in quality living. This does not in any way imply an affluence and preoccupation with things that sooner or later rob many of their very souls. The good life is that which is most conducive to serving both God and man. Our trouble in America since the mid-1940s has been one of gratification, satiation, and proliferation. We have tended in all areas of life to gratify desires quickly (even yesterday), satiate normal drives until we look like the proverbial "stuffed turkey," and proliferate in innumerable directions thinking all were beneficial.

God is not One to turn His back on basic material needs. The 23rd Psalm says, "The Lord is my shepherd, I shall not want." It is evident during our time that you and I are expected to be channels for meeting some of these needs. There are agencies of integrity through which we are working. The biggest factor is always our own attitude as we seek to do His will. Our Lord specifies the hungry, thirsty, stranger, naked, sick, and incarcerated. He may not be nearly as concerned about the food, water, hospitality, clothes, or visit as He is our willingness to be His servants and what it will do for us as we minister. Of course, there are the unscrupulous who will misuse, whatever we give them, but is it our mission to reform them before we do our Master's will?

IV.

You and I are called to be concise.

The Lord speaks again: "And in praying do not heap up empty phrases as the Gentiles do; for they think that they will be heard for their many words. Do not be like them, for your Father knows what you need before you ask him."

When we put it all together, we are expecting just five essentials from God: to control by a loving captivity; bestow righteous equity; provide spiritual prosperity; look after posterity; and grant material necessity.

Don't we have a right to expect all five from Him. I strongly believe we do. Surely you do as well. Won't you place them into your daily prayers?

CALLED TO BE FORGIVING
Matthew 6:14-15

I.

Life has its conditions, doesn't it?

We are taught from the time we are quite small that there are consequences to our actions. To touch a hot burner is to get burnt. To fall from a tree or down a flight of stairs is to get bruises and/or broken bones. To start across the street and get hit by an auto can result in dangerous injuries. To eat too much ice cream may give one a very large tummy ache. To get angry at a playmate is apt to cut off relations with him or her for a time. To get new clothes badly torn or severely soiled on the first day of school is likely to get a scolding from one or both parents. The list is almost exhaustive, isn't it? Sometimes the truth involved is so accurate we are led to conclude the percentage is 99% or more.

The same sort of dynamics is at work as long as we live. Educational level doesn't exempt us. Wealth will not change things, except perhaps on a temporary basis. The powerful have to live with their conditions just the same as the weak. In the professions and business, the higher one climbs the farther one can fall. That's an axiom that few, if any, are capable of altering. We know we are going to die or shed this physical form. Oh, in the teens and twenties we may think we are going to live in the current form forever, but in the thirties and forties we know better. Wisdom is a precious commodity and its chief function is to point out to us life's conditions.

We are brought now to a spiritual truth, on-going and ever-present.

The Lord (yours and mine) speaks about a very special condition or set of circumstances.

We turn to the sermon among sermons and discover the truth in the phrasing of Hebrews 4:12, "For the word of God is living and active, sharper than any two-edged sword . . ." Matthew 6:14-15 relays to us in one lengthy but distinct statement: "For if you forgive men their trespasses, your heavenly Father also will forgive you; but if you do not forgive men their trespasses, neither will your Father forgive your trespasses." Wow! That is quite a condition, isn't it? It's much like the wayfarer walking the beach of life absorbing the heat, kicking his toes in the sand, watching out for hurtful creatures, and then looking up to see a tidal wave too close to avoid.

I hope you will stay close to your God as we pursue the matter futher.

II.

You and I are called to be forgiving.

If we want forgiveness from the Father, we must grant it to our fellow pilgrims.

This assumes a certain style of living on our part. We could label it the Christian's triad. There are three closely related requirements.

III.

We have to be open and therefore vulnerable.
This runs the risk of being hurt, doesn't it? By nature you and I run from such a prospect. We may even set up a carefully constructed rationale for not taking the risk. We say, "Isn't there already enough hurt in the world?" We say, "It just isn't worth it. Life is too short." We say, "Let the other fellow take the chance of getting his brains beaten out. We're not going to." We say, "Our faith is idealistic and why not accept the realities of coming up short now and then?" While it is natural to flee from encounters

necessitating openness, our Lord brings us a salvation that removes this bent. Saint Paul says in Romans 6:6 "We know that our old self was crucified with Him so that the sinful body might be destroyed and we might no longer be enslaved to sin." Again, in Romans 12:2, the Apostle speaks: "Do not be conformed to this world but be transformed by the renewal of your mind, that you may prove what is the will of God, what is good and acceptable and perfect." We are reminded of the paraphrase of a famous Shakespearian line: "To be or not to be a Christian, that is the question."

Lest we begin to see a realistic approach to our lifestyle become overwhelmingly negative, let's pursue the realities of the floods of joy present in such living. Many of us grew up singing this hymn.

'Tis so sweet to trust in Jesus,
And to take him at his word;
Just to rest upon his promise,
And to know, "Thus saith the Lord."
Jesus, Jesus, how I trust him!
How I've proved him o'er and o'er!
Jesus, Jesus, precious Jesus!
O for grace to trust him more!

Yes, and on the opposite page in **The Book of Hymns** we see bursting from the page:

Be not dismayed whate'er betide,
God will take care of you;
Beneath his wings of love abide,
God will take care of you.
God will take care of you,
Through every day, o'er all the way'
He will take care of you,
God will take care of you.

To be crucified with Christ is to be resurrected with Him. Vulnerability and the real possibility of hurt? Yes. Victorious living and the promise of an imperishable crown? Yes! You and I are called to be forgiving, which is spelled out in continual crucifixions and resurrections, until the final resurrection into life eternal conquers all. Some Christians have an irrepressible glow about them precisely because they die with their Lord and live with their Lord on a daily basis.

Indeed, as you and I say to ourselves, "The Christian Faith will not work at the deeper levels," we are brought low by the voice that whispers, "Ah, but have you tried it?"

Now we are going to look at another part of the triad.

We have to be prayerful and, therefore, pious.

This means running the risk of appearing ridiculous, doesn't it? For centuries religious persons have had fun poked at them for being pious. Strong men have said weak men pray only because they cannot win at battle. The world has long depicted prayer as a pious pose for persons not knowing how to persist. Project yourself just now into the past shortly before the Crucifixion. Mark 15:17-19 records: "And they clothed him in a purple cloak, and plaiting a crown of thorns they put it on him. And they began to salute him, 'Hail, King of the Jews!' And they struck his head with a reed, and spat upon him, and they knelt down in homage to him." Yes, they did all of this and more to a pious Jew who commanded no army or navy. Only a little later this gentle Jew said, "Father, forgive them; for they know not what they do." (Luke 23:24) How did they respond to such a magnanimous utterance? Luke 23:35-36 relates: "And the people stood by, watching; but the rulers scoffed at him, saying, 'He saved others; let him save himself, if he is the Christ of God, his one.' " Then the

37th verse in the same chapter reports: "The soldiers also mocked him, coming up and offering him vinegar, and saying, 'If you are the King of the Jews, save yourself!' " Christ is our model. Are we brave enough to acknowledge our spiritual heritage?

Of course, those who have a strong prayer life know the strength that comes from forgiving others of their trespasses. The saints have witnessed to this fact for centuries. To be on our knees forgiving others who may have greatly wronged us captures in essence this requirement so filled with glorious feelings and peace of mind. Do you and I pray enough about matters that really count so that we can know firsthand the perfect harmony with God that comes to us through forgiving? In this matter of prayer in forgiving others, the Master has blessings untold ready to bestow. Have we sampled them lately? Christians are not just like everyone else. They forgive in prayer.

Repeatedly you and I attempt to be like the world. We are called to be forgiving. The world has a way of never quite forgiving anyone of anything. John Wesley has a famous sermon entitled "The Almost Christian." Should he preach it to you and me?

A final part of the triad beckons. It puts the finishing touches to a lifestyle called forth by the text. It, too, is required.

We have to be compassionate and therefore tender.

In this case we run the risk of appearing weak. The world does not respect weakness. To show care and concern for others always involves the opportunity for the so-called strong to level avalanches of criticism. Compare our time with that of the early portion of the First Century. The Roman Empire was great, mighty, and victorious. The Christ, His Apostles, and disciples were quite the opposite. The Roman administrators ran a successful operation, so to speak; but at times it was harsh, cruel, and totally inhuman. A small band loyal to "the" Galilean was quite a contrast. The difference was largely their call to be forgiving, which they made a part of their lives. While you and I cherish our American citizenship, it is well for us to remember our Lord's response to Pilate: "My kingship is not of this world." (John 18:36) The world again and again indicates the only right way to redress a grievance is by getting back at wrongdoers, either subtly, or most directly through the judicial system. To forgive is for the weak is the dictum.

If there were not Christians taking their Faith seriously by showering compassion on others, what chance does the human race have of continuing? You and I know the answer to that one, don't we? When "the chips are down," we know very well the point our Lord is making. We also hopefully know the hope and joy that can be known this way. Our Faith does not give priority to those matters that are trivial, which the world pictures as highly significant. Our priorities are nearly, maybe completely, in reverse order to those outside of the Faith. The purity of the Methodist societies in the 18th Century testify to this reassuring fact. A major criterion for staying in one of those societies was: "By doing good; by being in every kind merciful after their power; as they have opportunity, doing good of every possible sort, and, as far as possible, to all men." Among other imperatives John Wesley interprets this to mean:

> By running with patience the race which is set before them, denying themselves, and taking up their cross daily; submitting to bear the reproach of Christ, to be as the filth and off scouring of the world; and looking that men should say all manner of evil of them falsely, for the Lord's sake.

So, compassion is a directive from Christ that should not bend at the whims of anemic Christians. When it is absent, there is no forgiveness. In short, we cannot fulfill our call by leaving it out of our lives. Praise God for a Faith that has such a stringent but superlative essential!

IV.

From the first time we accepted the Lord, we were called to be forgiving.

Hear Him once more: "For if you forgive men their trespasses, your heavenly Father also will forgive you; but if you do not forgive men their trespasses, neither will your Father forgive your trespasses."

A certain lifestyle virtually leaps from the words: We have to be open and, therefore, vulnerable; prayerful and, therefore, pious; and compassionate and, therefore, tender.

Let's you and I join together just now and forgive everyone who has wronged us.

There is great power in this. You and I need to perform this healing act in order to continue our upward climb. Indeed, the doldrums in the Christian life are often characterized by an unforgiving spirit. I challenge you to withhold your forgiveness from no one. We feel better already, don't we?

I earnestly, even like a child, want the Father's forgiveness, don't you? We know how to get it. As individuals and as a church we should have turned a corner during this brief moment . . . and heaven is at stake!

CALLED TO BE UNPRETENTIOUS
Matthew 6:16

I.

In recent years the youth of our nation have done us a lasting service by exposing phoniness.

Their young hearts and minds seem to regurgitate every time a calloused adult puts on a different mask. This is not to say such youth are imbued with perfect morality. It is to say they have the affinity for seeing a person attempting to be something he or she wasn't . . . and with clarity. They are the prophets of the sixties and early seventies that count candor of utmost importance. They show those a generation or two older that the games played on all levels could lead only to greater hypocrisy and, in time, outright mental illness. The point: after a while one becomes incapable of distinguishing the right from the wrong. Then the most treacherous and destructive schizophrenia comes into existence. No person or body of people can afford to allow that to happen. Decadence cannot be far away with such forces at work. Praise God, He applies correctives! We are a better people for the youth who reveal our sick ways.

Isn't it fascinating (and inspiring) how God rescues us individually and collectively? There are major turning points. I, for one, believe the picture just depicted of the pure integrity of our youth was one. We are too close to prove this historically. Yet, there is that special kind of feeling and mental alertness that tells us we were forced to be honest or at least see our pretensions and are better people because of it. The rescuing party may not have been to our liking. In fact, the purifying waters may have scalded a bit.

Our Lord makes clear that religious pretending has no rightful place in the Faith.

In Matthew 6:16 He deals with it head-on: "And when you fast, do not look dismal, like the hypocrites, for they disfigure their faces that their fasting may be seen by men. Truly, I say to you, they have their reward." Jesus is speaking about those who wear masks, isn't He? There is a repugnance about them. They are trying to be something or someone they aren't. Note that our Lord assumes His followers will fast. He doesn't want them just to yield to the temptation that gives an impression fraught with hypocrisy when they do so.

Health and well-being are tied directly to the Christian and interwoven most certainly within the Christian by our Lord's call to be unpretentious.

II.

Religious pretending today is no different from our Lord's day.

There are easily recognizable signs. You and I do not have to be experts or even saints. So, just how do we spot phoniness?

III.

Gross exaggeration is the first sign.

Comic routines for generations have been built on this. Bob Hope, Red Skelton, Jack Benny, Milton Berle, and Lucille Ball, are excellent illustrations. People laughed, guffawed, and chuckled as people and situations became funny through a great deal of exaggerating. They were masters.

In the Master's time there were those who were tragically comical. They went without food and wanted to be sure everyone noticed they looked dismal; they disfigured their faces. They wanted everyone to know they were doing something religiously important. Yes, they must have put on quite an act. Our Lord says they have their reward! They took a meaningful spiritual discipline, grossly exaggerated it, and caused people to snicker at their hypocrisy.

Jesus is saddened by those who advertise their piety. Oh, it isn't that abstinence from food is the problem. It's the matter of drawing attention to oneself and in one way or several saying, "Look at me. I'm really doing something great for God." Jesus Himself fasted, but I would be surprised if anyone ever knew it, except those closest to Him.

Do you and I take some lovely things and blow them completely out of proportion? Do we give the impression we are in worship every Sunday . . . when in reality we aren't there even 50% of the time? Do we give the impression we are indispensable to the financial structure of the church . . . when in reality our giving is on a temperamental basis, if at all? Do we give the impression we give long hours in service to the church . . . when in reality we baked a pie last year for a dinner or ushered once during the summer?

There's more to phoniness, isn't there?

Deliberate falsification is the second sign.

Communism has been adept at attempts to falsify the Faith. Knowingly, cunningly, and calculatingly it has put symbols of atheistic materialism in places that should have been occupied by the cross or the fish. It has put black robes and the clerical collar on men dedicated to communistic victory. It has called black white and white black so often in some countries the people succumb in confusion. Then they are prepared to swallow large doses of hellish indoctrination.

In our own society we witness those who methodically and diabolically set out to depict a person or group something that is a serious misrepresentation. Some innocent people can be destroyed this way. Such hypocrisy always has an odor about it. If our nostrils can detect it in time, we are indeed fortunate.

Our Blessed Lord had to deal with such a problem. In fact the charge that seemed to carry the most weight was the label "imposter." Many said He pretended to be something he was not. Collusion against Him was common, especially in the latter weeks of His ministry, culminating in the kiss of Judas Iscariot. To falsify deliberately is to betray.

Have you and I sought to place persons in a light that would make them look like something they are not? If we have done so, why? Could it be in order to reduce them to our levels? Could it be we aren't very concerned about the forward movement of the Church and don't want anyone else to be?

Blessed be the God of our Lord and Savior Jesus the Christ, He does guide us and lead us above the dismal and disfigured faces that would hold down spiritual growth! We serve the risen Lord, in time always victorious. We love Him because He first loved us.

Let's look to another mark of mischief.

Contrived appreciation is the third sign.

We have all been thanked and complimented profusely. Sometimes it's just like a "noisy gong or a clanging cymbal." In the vernacular it is a "snow job." We wonder how some can keep from choking on the words that come forth with insincerity. We may not know the reasons, but we certainly can observe the fabricated praise.

The cliche "if you can't say something good about somebody, don't say it" is not a spiritual gem out of Holy Writ, but it bears repeating. We all like to be appreciated. However, there is an integrity involved. Words of honest appreciation are born from emotions kindled by gratitude with a mind that is in agreement. Emotional expression and a disengaged mind can get us into woeful predicaments!

There is a philosophy today that says, "It doesn't make any difference whether you want to pay compliments or not. Go ahead and fake it." I cannot buy into that. In my opinion the end result of that is little different from what Jesus is pointing out to us in the text. We ask for new problems and solve none of the old ones. We say things we know we don't mean. I do not see how spiritual health can be improved that way. In fact quite the reverse seems to be true.

In the life of the Church we are to appreciate one another. Praise God, in a majority of cases we do! Let's say so! Our Lord and Savior is not One who leaves us unguided. If need be, let's fall upon our knees and talk the matter over with Him. He will give a listening ear to our falling into the trap of contriving appreciation. Sincerity is given birth at the time we receive Him. It is Satan who wants us to cut corners and compromise an integrity that comes with our conversion.

We must move ahead.

Awkward application is the fourth sign.

Counterfeit money isn't spendable. There is something that is not right about it. It doesn't fit. It doesn't belong in the flow of legitimate currency. To be caught manufacturing it or trafficking in it is a serious offense. Of course, it may take an expert to determine its lack of authenticity.

One of the first things a pastor of a church must learn is to listen closely and observe carefully. This is especially true in the context of a local church which is an organism. Sometimes it malfunctions, not quite in the sense that fewer parts are being produced or defective products are causing the plant manager sleepless nights. Even though a church must be administered in a businesslike way to a large extent, it is never a business as popularly understood. At any rate, the pastor must be alert to what's happening to the body of believers, even those who are nominal in commitment. An awkwardness in the life of God's people may signal that someone or group is attempting to apply unworthy principles, which is often a matter of seeking unwarranted power and questionable prestige. A church can be a tottering old person lacking creativity and the will to plan for the future. It can also be a reckless youth with no thought of preservation and essential organization.

So, there are times we can sense or know there is something awry. It can be a matter of religious pretending. In 2 Timothy 3:5 it says, "Hold the form of religion but denying the power of it. Avoid such people."

A final time we deal with detecting phoniness. **Crass implication is the fifth sign.**

One of the new words to make the dictionaries in recent years is McCarthyism. It is defined as an "attitude characterized chiefly by opposition to elements held to be subversive by the use of tactics involving personal attacks on individuals by means of widely publicized indiscriminate allegations, especially on the basis of unsubstantiated charges." It is obvious such a mind set is still operative today and it is the possession of no single group. Of course, it is not new to the world. The intrigues of every European court for centuries knew and perfected the process.

In the life of the Church, innuendos make us look like the world. When this happens, it is a day of sorrows. Repentance is desperately needed and quickly. To allow just a few sick words leave our mouths can and does set off a chain reaction. Implying negative things about persons that are untrue or halftrue is crassness most at home in the lower region of hell. Can't we hear Christ saying, "You were called to bear My name, but look at you!"

Our Lord has no room for the camouflaged stick of dynamite in His Body. Let's not pretend so-and-so is guilty of crimes that are fictions brewed and stewed in Satan's kitchen.

Hence, we now begin to conclude our visit together.

IV.

Those many centuries ago Christ called His people to be unpretentious.

It is the same today. The genius of His way is its undying relevance. Praise be to God we have that way preserved in Holy Scripture!

Lend an ear again to His Word to us this day: "And when you fast, do not look dismal, like the hypocrites, for they disfigure their faces that their fasting may be seen by man. Truly, I say to you, they have their reward."

The signs of religious pretending are at least five in number: gross exaggeration, deliberate falsification, contrived appreciation, awkward application, and crass implication.

Can others look at us and say without doubt, "There is the real McCoy. That person is a Christian, if ever I've seen one"? To have that said is more than a fine compliment; it is saying we have touched the hem of the Master's garment and others are rightfully impressed. The disciples of Christ are called to be unpretentious; that includes you and me.

CALLED TO BE THRIFTY
Matthew 6:19-21

I.

Many people have difficulty distinguishing between being thrifty and being stingy.

The difference is one of far-reaching consequences. Thrift is a matter of careful management. When necessity is obvious, it is generous. When real need beckons, it is the first to share. It takes stewardship seriously, theoretically and practically. Life, property, and talents are a gift from God. "Waste" is a bad word. Gorging oneself with possessions is avoided. If "bigger barns are built" it is because there is a noble purpose for doing so. Thrift requires that life be lived well under the discipline of recognizing God's absolute ownership. Now, to be stingy is something quite different. It is a matter of prolonged introversion that tends to have one motto: That's mine and I am going to keep it. Children below the age of six are not very sharing. They usually want to gain, keep, and control. Stinginess builds its own world of continually saving for "rainy days" even when the sun has been shining for years. It is a point of view that robs everyone, especially the practitioner.

How do you see yourself? Into which of the two categories do you fall? Most of us, in my opinion, fall predominantly into one or the other. A great deal depends on our trust in God and love for one another, especially those within the Household of Faith. John Donne said it so well in one of his meditations: "No man is an Island intire of itselfe; every man is a peece of the Continent, a part of the maine . . ." How very true that is as we interact with one another in the Faith! It seems to me stinginess is in direct opposition to the teachings of our Lord. While Christians from the beginning have been known as strong individuals, they have also been known as such in the context of a group. Discipleship infers meaningful relationships with other Christians. A disciple is expected to be thrifty, but can he or she be stingy?

Christ points the way to spiritual thrift.

In the memorable passage of Matthew 6:19-21, He teaches us: "Do not lay up for yourselves treasures on earth, where moth and rust consume and where thieves break in and steal, but lay up for yourselves treasures in heaven, where neither moth nor rust consumes and where thieves do not break in and steal. For where your treasure is there will your heart be also." What a statement of spiritual thrift! We are called to be thrifty. Heaven is the depository and is directly connected to what happens here and now.

Our Lord intends that we see the verses as a unity. Verse 21 has been used to mean all sorts of things and, I am afraid, not by the most conscientious. Our call to be thrifty surfaces from all three verses.

II.

For the Christian, real accumulation takes place in heaven. With care, he or she deposits. With love, he or she wants others to do likewise.

This means we are to view and accept the walk with Christ as being four-dimensional.

III.

A willingness to gain money as well as lose it is the first dimension.

At first this sounds strange, doesn't it? Surely to be on both ends of gaining and losing money is not an ideal situation for thrift to play an important part. We think of thrift in the context of building up a nest egg and then utilizing it with great care. It is only as we push ourselves into a dimension where actual gain or loss of money is of slight consequence that we begin to understand what Christ means by laying up treasures in heaven. Then we discover thrift is of crucial importance because it is with great care we look after these treasures.

We have all read about or know the person who lost a fortune and then committed suicide. He or she could not tolerate relinquishing the grip of a material that contained the basic meaning of life for him or her. While such illustrations are classic, the more depressing occurrences are those who, in their daily walk, chase rainbows painted in many shades of currency. The treasure is spelled out in dollar signs. If they eventually arrive at the point of wealth, the moth and rust will most assuredly consume and thieves will break in and steal. There is no bank account ever big enough to withstand such destruction, because it comes into being for the wrong reasons. Of course, if a person can lose all materially and grow in the grace of our Lord, then we have, spiritually speaking, an ideal situation. It becomes that magnificent picture of a person losing the temporary and gaining the eternal.

Making, saving, and even piling up money in our society is not necessarily bad . . . unless the person would be destroyed by losing it. Ask the visceral or gut question: Can I lose a large portion of it or even all of it, and still shout the praises of my Lord and Savior? It seems to me that Christ, telling us to lay up treasures in heaven, makes it clear we must be willing to gain or lose money. We all remember, some from our earliest days, the story of the rich young ruler. He asked, apparently with sincerity, what he could do to inherit eternal life. After hearing about his lofty moral living, Jesus said, "You lack one thing; go sell what you have, and give it to the poor, and you will have treasure in heaven; and come, follow me." (Mark 10:21) Note Jesus does **not** say if he meets the requirement, he is to remain penniless the rest of his days; He says, ". . . come, follow me."

We are just beginning to enter a blessed and exciting spiritual realm, so let's not tarry.

A willingness to gain friends as well as lose them is the second dimension.

Friendship is hard to define, isn't it? Every book of famous quotations lists several, each slightly different. Sometimes it seems to be built on love and respect at the deepest levels. Other times it seems to be a matter of expediency.

The Christian is secure in his or her Faith in which friends may come and go without destroying that Faith. The real concern is invariably treasures in heaven. To lose a friend is not the end of the world. It may be the inception of a new and far better world in which Christ is King. To be forsaken by a lifelong friend hurts, but our Lord says, in Hebrews 13:5, "I will never fail you nor forsake you." As the stormy waves toss about us and we remain steadfast in the Lord, we know treasures are securely tucked away in heaven. Then it dawns on us that our call to be thrify is in reality a precious conserving of that which no one, not even the palace guard in hell, can diminish in any way whatsoever.

I recently read that a prominent pulpiteer said, "The trouble with too many preachers is that they preach sermons and not Christ." There is a radiant truth about that and it should cause all of us who stand behind pulpits regularly to listen carefully and not run from the fruitful message. I would add this revision: The trouble with too many laypersons is that they live in conformity with what their fleeting friends prescribe and refuse to live as Christ would have them live. In both cases, we attempt to lay up treasures on earth. There is only one way to practice thrift as

Christians in the ultimate sense and that is to put our rubies, diamonds, emeralds, and other precious gems where they can continue to sparkle and glow in a myriad of spectacular ways; that, my comrades in Christ, is in heaven.

Come with me a step further.

A willingness to rise in the world's sight as well as to fall is the third dimension.

"The world loves a winner" is in evidence every day. Who is lauded to the skies? The winner. Who is given the most attention and praised the loudest? The winner. What is ingrained in being a winner? Position, power, and dollars. Can a man, woman, or youth fail and still receive praises from the world? Maybe, but probably not. The world loves to be a part of winning and generally is unkind to losers.

Now, it is not fair for us to say Christ demands we lose in the game of life in order to spend eternity with Him. He may lead us into pathways of prominence. We may receive local or even world acclaim. On different occasions there were those who gave Him standing ovations. However, remember when the world saw He would not be successful in their terms, they castigated Him and, in effect, told Him to get lost. To win or lose in the sight of the world may or may not be His will for our lives. The point is we are His and He is ours; we have Him in success and we have Him in failure.

As we move higher in the Faith that glorious door opens signifying we need neither approval nor disapproval of the world to be strong, sturdy Christians. We have seen those who bend easily with the winds of the world. Steadfast Christians should look after them. A "make or break" situation is especially noticeable in the early period of one's walk with the Master or a return to Him after disowning Him. Saint Paul begins the third chapter of 1 Corinthians by saying, "But I brethren, could not address you as spiritual men, but as men of the flesh, as babes in Christ." "Babes in Christ," of course, are at all ages. Satan, if possible, will keep them in diapers and prevent the maturing Christ intends.

Thrift, under the banner of the Galilean, takes success and failure in stride as the world applauds or belittles. The spiritual fortune of which the Lord speaks remains untouched. Indeed, the Christian knows where his or her treasure is. The call to be thrifty was and is heeded.

One more time we are going to look at a dimension.

A willingness to rise in the Church or Body of Believers as well as to fall is the fourth dimension.

In the closing segment of John Wesley's covenant service it says:

I am no longer my own, but thine.
Put me to what thou wilt,
rank me with whom thou wilt;
put me to doing, put me to suffering;
let me be employed for thee or laid aside for
     thee,
exalted for thee or brought low for thee;
let me be full, let me be empty;
let me have all things, let me have nothing;
I freely and heartily yield all things to thy
pleasure and disposal.

These lines from that moving and penetrating service hold up for all to see the call to be thrifty. Regardless of what happens as long as one is in Christ, one's treasure in heaven is preserved and receiving dividends. What we sometimes fail to recognize — and with the possibility of jeopardizing our spiritual growth — is that this applies to the life of the Church. John Wesley's own career took him in and out of the institutional Church. He was abused by brothers of the cloth and in fact found pulpits closed to him. This was true in spite of the fact he lived and died as a priest in the Church of England.

The jewels in our crowns grow in number as we move, sometimes not too gracefully, from position to position and relationship to relationship. We may not see ourselves at the helm of a particular committee, but God does. We may not like the thought of becoming less visible in the leadership of a Church, but this is God's way. God's will transcends ours and yet it works on our behalf infinitely more than we could. To be brought low in the institutional Church may very well mean to rise to heights previously unknown in heaven. Of course, to be elevated to a pinnacle of manifest power does not of necessity mean one's soul has been auctioned off to the highest bidder. All experience in the Body of Believers is intended for our good.

In one of John Wesley's prayers he says, "O God, who by thy Holy Spirit didst at first establish a Church, and who, sanctifying it by the same Spirit, dost still preserve and govern it. . ."

IV.

Isn't it remarkable the way the Master calls you and me to be thrifty?

His people have the unique distinction of laying up for themselves that which refuses to perish. Praise His holy Name! Thank You, Lord, thank You!

Write all three verses into your innermost being and never for one instant allow them to be forgotten: "Do not lay up for yourselves treasures on earth, where moth and rust consume and where thieves break in and steal, but lay up for yourselves treasures in heaven, where neither moth nor rust consumes and where thieves do not break in and steal. For where your treasure is, there will your heart be also."

There are four dimensions in this highest call to be thrifty: a willingness to gain money or lose it; to gain friends or lose them; to rise in the world's sight or fall; and to rise in the Church or fall.

Have we now begun to understand what it means to be called to be thrifty? You may be young, old, or someplace between. It is never too early or too late to answer the call.

CALLED TO BE 20/20
Matthew 6:22-23

I.

Eyesight is a precious gift from God.

I suppose none of us who has had reasonably good seeing faculties over the years can really imagine what it is like to be blind. Yet, let's try to envision some beautiful things that would go unseen. All of us have seen the dawning of a new day. As the sun begins to rise and fill the morning with light and promise, we know the Creator God is majestically on His throne. A child sits on the street corner weeping because his dog has been run over. Our eyesight causes us to feel compassion, and we even feel inclined to sit down and cry with him. A jolly, elderly lady walks along and smiles, greeting people with a radiance only God can bestow. She celebrated her eightieth birthday only a few weeks ago. Suppose we could not see any of these touching sights. If you are like I am, I can imagine only because I have witnessed such things all my days.

Like so many other things, we take eyesight for granted. In our prayers we should specifically now and then say, "God, thank You, for this marvelous ability to see Your creation." Then from time to time, when so much of what some of us do is dependent on reading, we should kneel — not stand — and pray, "Oh, God, thank You for allowing my work to continue because of eyesight." It has been said we do not actually appreciate something until we have either lost it or almost lost it. There is more than a small amount of truth in that. Gratitude moves us forward and upward in the Faith. Won't you thank Him and continue to do so for the blessing of seeing?

Our Lord teaches and tantalizes us with some concepts about the eyes and seeing.

In Matthew 6:22-23, the Master gives to us frankly an intriguing, almost mystifying, word: "The eye is the lamp of the body. So, if your eye is sound, your whole body will be full of light; but if your eye is not sound, your whole body will be full of darkness. If then the light in you is darkness, how great is the darkness!" He puts the message beyond our fingertips and motions for us to probe into the richness of what is said. I visualize a gleam in His eye.

In our own weak and incomplete way, what translates to us, at least, part of what He is conveying? Spiritually speaking, the Christian is to have topflight vision. He or she is called to be 20/20.

II.

The Christian who sees with clarity, or 20/20 vision, focuses on three spiritual realities. A diseased or defective eye is incapable of providing this. In fact it will even cause what light we have to be distorted into twilight or darkness.

So, let us affirm and live victoriously with what we are intended as Christians to see all our days that darkness may not blight our souls.

III.

The first spiritual reality is that Christians see opportunities and not problems.
This is born knowing all things are possible with God. Saint Paul says in Philippians 4:14, "I can do all things in him who strengthens me." Do you and I ever really pause long enough in prayer and meditation to acknowledge the splendor and comfort involved in such truth? Just think of it! **All** things are possible with God. You and I belong to God through His Son, Jesus the Christ. If we believed that with all our heart, mind, soul, and strength, what sort of a Church would we

be? We are in touch with the Almighty! Why settle for a few sparks now and then when the most powerful of all generators is at our fingertips?

To see with 20/20 vision is to look at a situation long enough to recognize the opportunity or opportunities present. Wasn't it this manner of ministry that Jesus showed us? I definitely think so. The sick were healed. The guilty were forgiven. The hypocrites were warned. Saint Paul eloquently proclaims in Romans 8:38-39, "For I am sure that neither death nor life nor angels, nor principalities, nor things present, nor things to come, nor powers, nor height, nor depth, nor anything else in all creation, will be able to separate us from the love of God in Christ Jesus our Lord." Are you and I able to affirm that statement of undying faith with the Apostle? Let's challenge one another often to leave behind a tendency to tip the Church with our hats and/or pocketbooks merely to maintain an artificial sign of religious devotion.

Perhaps the most tragic of all lives is the one terminated never knowing the riches found in our first spiritual reality. In today's world the perverting of such a reality into a manipulative pragmatism seeking only one's selfish advantage is an enormous stumbling block. Sometimes that's what is wrong with the simplistic "power of positive thinking." It makes the blessings of God — yes, even His sovereignty — fall into the category of the cleverness of human and secular ingenuity. Go to your Bibles, read and study them. Take them to your beings and love them as the Word of God because, after all, that's what they are.

On May 21, 1739, Charles Wesley wrote one of his 6,500 hymns. It was the anniversary of his conversion. The first line goes:

O for a thousand tongues to sing
My great Redeemer's praise

The glories of my God and King,
The triumphs of his grace!

Do you and I sing these lines, sensing and knowing the powerful love imbedded? Charles Wesley knew that Christians see opportunities and not problems. Why? Because God through Christ makes us new creatures, refusing the world's way of wanting to use the Faith for base reasons.

For a moment we are going to look at a portion of the greatness of Martin Luther's legacy. His universally sung hymn tells us:

Did we in our own strength confide,
Our striving would be losing,
Were not the right man on our side
The man of God's own choosing:
Dost ask who that may be?
Christ Jesus it is he;
Lord Sabaoth, his name
From age to age the same,
And he must win the battle.

To rely on our own strength is to be defeated. To belong to Christ makes all the difference. To belong to Him is to discover the meaninglessness of problems and the truth of perpetual opportunity.

Are we beginning to know how well we see?
Come and learn more in our quest together.

The second spiritual reality is that Christians see life as a gift and not an acquisition.

There is a huge difference in that which is given to us and that which we acquire. To worship and serve God is made possible in the most elementary sense by the sheer fact He has given life to us. It is a privilege to be in a sanctuary worshiping God. It is a privilege to serve Him and one another on Sunday and every other day. Drudgery in one's religious experience is often, if not always, a negative matter because the Christian sees his or her existence in the context of acquiring good feelings or a better image. Such a joyless style of practicing the Faith recalls the attempts by many over the ages to place works before faith and never actually see the complete interdependence of the two. An unhappy Christian over a long period of time, especially one who is very cognizant of keeping a rigid agenda to make and keep him or her a Christian, sees Christ as a demanding Lord that places works over faith. Could it be we are "works-oriented" Pharisees and Sadducees?

Every day that you and I have is given from above. In a less mechanized and unhurried time we remembered that all-pervasive truth much better. Nevertheless, we should not bewail the times into which we are born. God controls that, too. Do we ever stop to ponder that, after all, God wanted us born in the latter part of the 19th or the 20th Century or we wouldn't be here? God could have placed us in the 17th or some other century. I knew an old fellow, nearly devoid of this world's goods, who would awaken each morning and say to his Maker, "Well, I'm still here. Thank you, Lord." Regardless of our educational level, money, and social standing that's as much as you and I can say each morning. When we sift and sort our theological bag, sooner or later in essence we say to the God of all creation, "I'm still here. Thank you, God." We certainly don't stay here without His approval! We did not and do not acquire this life.

God, in particular through His Son the Christ, spreads before us life and its vast potential for good. Christians thank Him and revel in the joy that abounds in being a full-fledged disciple of Christ. To profess His name — indeed to shout it or whisper it — is a living testimony. "Every day with Jesus is sweeter than the day before" is more than a catchy jingle. It verbalizes the feeling of one immersed in life and praising God for each additional day. Many of the revival meetings of old held high the gift of living to Christians who witnessed to the world and one another with the marvels found in simply being alive one day at a time in Christ.

How are we doing in seeing spiritual reality by now?

A final time we are going to check our eyesight.

The third spiritual reality is that Christians see Jesus the Christ as Savior and Lord and not as just another talented religious leader.

As has often been said in the study of religions, this is the reality that sets Christianity apart from the others. Every major religion in the world of which I am aware sees Jesus as a religious leader with talent. You and I might be able to practice several religions simultaneously, except for the imperative of Jesus as Lord and Savior. There are those in today's world who claim they pick and choose from Hinduism, Islam, Buddhism, and the others. Scholars call this an eclectic approach, which is the process of selecting the best from each and weaving them together in a workable style of living. It has a tempting aroma to it. This is so true; there are those who worship from a world bible, which is composed of sacred writings from a number of religions.

To our foregoing elaboration, Saint Peter filled with the Holy Spirit would and does say in Acts 4:12, "And there is salvation in no other name under heaven given among men by which we must be saved." That is one of the boldest and most direct statements in the entire Bible. One has to have terrible eyesight not to be able to see it. In the same chapter, Jewish leaders warned Peter and John "not to speak or teach at all in the name of Jesus." They responded with the best answer any of us can give:

"Whether it is right in the sight of God to listen to you rather than to God, you must judge; for we cannot but speak of what we have seen and heard."

Jesus Himself says in the Gospel of John, "I am the way, and the truth, and the life; no one comes to the Father, but by me. If you had known me, you would have known my Father also; henceforth you know him and have seen him." (14:6-7) If you and I "receive and profess the Christian faith as contained in the Scriptures of the Old and New Testaments," I do not know how much more plainly it can be said. Of course, if we choose to take scissors and past to the Book of Life, we can come up with most anything. Article V of "The Articles of Religion of the Methodist Church" (1784) says, "The Holy Scripture containeth all things necessary to salvation . . ." Article IV of "The Confession of Faith of the Evangelical United Brethren Church" says, "We believe the Holy Bible, Old and New Testaments, reveals the Word of God so far as it is necessary for our salvation."

So, we near the end of a topic always essential to our spiritual growth and well-being.

IV.

The Christian is called to be 20/20. Spiritual eyesight counts! What we see makes all the difference in our existence. We cannot go around with poor vision and expect to see others, ourselves, and our God in terms of noble purpose, inherent worth, and intended wholeness. Diseased and defective vision destroys and/or distorts the significance of that which is within us because we never know where or who we are.

The Lord's Word is eternally profound: "The eye is the lamp of the body. So, if your eye is sound, your whole body will be full of light; but if your eye is not sound, your whole body will be full of darkness. If then the light in you is darkness, how great is the darkness!"

There are three spiritual realities or life-giving and affirming threads that unfold: Christians see opportunities and not problems; life as a gift and not an acquisition; and Jesus the Christ as Lord and Savior and not as just another talented religious leader.

How well do you and I see? When Christ became our Savior and Lord, He gave us new powers for seeing with accuracy both inwardly and outwardly, didn't He? Glory, glory, hallelujah, our Faith is one of light and not darkness one of seeing spiritual realities that make all twenty-four hours of every day truly worth living!

CALLED TO BE SINGLE-MINDED
Matthew 6:24

I.

The First of the Ten Commandments is potently profound, overshadowing the others.

Exodus rings with thunder from Mount Sinai: "You shall have no other gods before me." (20:3) This one sets the tone for those that follow. No person, animal, ideology, or thing is to come between a human being and God. The Commandment is made up of one- and two-syllable words. It cannot be mistaken. It moves to us with such divine directness and overpowering simplicity that it cannot be misunderstood. "That's the way it is," says our God, "and you take it lightly at your eternal peril." There is an awesomeness about it all upon which hangs your destiny and mine. Someone has said cynically with some derision, "Yes, the initial command of Moses is the Hebrew hard sell" to which you and I should reply, "Take off your shoes! You have entered hallowed ground and you treat it like a chimpanzee puttering around disrespectfully in a magnificent garden."

The survival and sanity of humanity are tied to this Commandment. Mankind will have a god or gods of some sort. I suppose everything published in the social sciences would sooner or later confirm that statement. We have a need — not extractable — to look to a higher power within and without. No one or no generation of people can remain sane and ignore it. Perhaps the best of examples in this century thus far was the Nazi regime in Germany.

By now you may be saying to yourselves, "All well and good. We agree, but where do we go from here in a brief time frame?" Well, we move from the Old to the New Testament. We look to our Lord for a pointed directive.

Jesus the Christ builds upon this Commandment in a specific sense.

In Matthew 6:24, He proclaims a principle, piercing and pertinent: "No one can serve two masters; for either he will hate the one and love the other, or he will be devoted to the one and despise the other. You cannot serve God and mammon." We are called to be single-minded. We cannot have other gods before Him — in particular mammon — which translates into "riches" or material wealth. He does not say we have to be poverty-stricken to worship and serve God. He says to place mammon ahead of God means we cannot possibly serve God.

The call to be single-minded is to the Christian. Are we heeding the call? Will we?

II.

Christians who go all the way in the Faith are unique and an exception to the main currents of the world and some of the currents within the institutional Church. They hear a different drummer and His name is Jesus the Christ. We can elucidate by looking into four distinctive responses they make to their environment.

Such Christians wonder sometimes why they don't fit in as the world views happenings and events. Whoever said they would? You and I are called to be single-minded and that means **one** Master, God.

III.

The first response is they have power in circumstances that others are powerless.

What do we mean by this? Simply, God's love is the most powerful force in the entire universe. To those who are born anew He grants love in more colors than have ever been in all the rainbows put together. When asked which was the first of the commandments, His reply was, in effect, a final and fulfilling restatement of the first one given at Mount Sinai. He said, "The first is, 'Hear, O Israel: The Lord our God, the Lord is one; and you shall love the Lord your God with all your heart, with all your soul, and with all your mind, and with all your strength.' " (Mark 12:31) The power generated in those lines is beyond our comprehension. Christians have direct access to it not because of their goodness but because of God's greatness evidenced in love.

The power which comes to us and works within us is due to our identity. 1 John 3:2 glows with glory: "Beloved, we are God's children now; it does not yet appear what we shall be but we know that when he appears we shall be like him, for we shall see him as he is." The Christian does not have an identity crisis, unless it is produced by an unwillingness to grow. The growing Christian knows who he or she is. Why fritter away our lives by playing the guessing game, "Who am I?" In love we belong to God. Saint Paul tells us, in 1 Corinthians 6:19-20, that ". . .You are not your own; you were bought with a price."

Are some muttering under their breath, "Preacher, that sounds good, but I don't know what you are talking about?" Your Lord and Savior says, "And I tell you, ask, and it will be given you; seek, and you will find; knock, and it will be opened to you." (Luke 11:9) Then He comes back in the very next verse in the same chapter and says, "For everyone who asks receives, and he who seeks finds, and to him who knocks it will be opened." Do you find that difficult to believe? Don't you think it is more difficult not to believe it?

Heeding the call to be single-minded brings to our attention something else peculiar to Christians.

The second response is they radiate purpose in situations that others find purposeless.

The Master says it so well and succinctly early in the Sermon on the Mount: "You are the salt of the earth . . ." (Matthew 5:13) Isn't that exciting? In the eyes of the world it looks like an ego trip. For those who are single-minded in serving one Master it is a natural course of events. We are the saving feature in situations. That doesn't mean we smooth out the rough places necessarily. There are those who regard anything less than 100% acceptance of their ideas as being ungodly. As a sage said, "Some persons will pay large sums for health and happiness; but they will give away everything they own to get their way." As Christians we are never always right; we bear witness to being in the right. Remembering the difference between the two often spells out failure or success in Christ's Kingdom.

During the years of my ministry I have observed numerous Christians who devalued and thwarted their Faith. There was so much more within them, but they refused to let the healing rays loose. Satan's subtle and sincere way of telling us, "Now you don't want to appear foolish" bears fruit. Too late we learn it is not only sour and beginning to rot, but wormeaten as well. You and I do not come on like selfrighteous gangbusters showing others how brilliant we are and how much of Christ we have. We don't have to do that. Our call is to be single-minded and that simply means we serve one Master. His name is Jesus the Christ.

In a day when people are constantly touching wills and spirits in a grating way, we learn just to be together largely in quietude may be more important than to come to any earthshaking decisions. The unhurried, unplanned, and unsophisticated inter-action of precious sons and daughters of the Father may provide more real food for ongoing vital living than heavy agendas and hour-long reports. There is a word with which you may be familar. It is **koinonia**, a Greek word. In an elementary sense it indicates a fellowship or sharing of Christians with the spirit of Christ present. The small group movement around the world in recent years gives example after example. There may be no greater purpose than just coming together as Christians. Then, to use a play on words, we rediscover purpose and take it into situations others find purposeless.

Taking to our hearts and minds, indeed our very wills, the call to be single-minded causes us to look again at the distinctiveness of Christians.

The third response is they accept privilege in circles that others consider unprivileged.

While we tend to feel more comfortable with those in the same economic and social categories, our Faith transcends and works through such imposing barriers. To have the mind of Christ is to move freely among all classes. The 1st Century Church dealt with the partiality issue in the Epistle of James. The second chapter tells of a man with gold rings and fine clothing and a poor man in shabby clothing. One is asked to please have a seat and the other is told to stand or sit at someone's feet. Distinctions of this type are seen as coming from a judgmental attitude with evil thoughts. In the same chapter, James relates point-blank, "But if you show partiality, you commit sin, and are convicted by the law as transgressors." (2:9) To be "one in Christ" is to obliterate that which separates and divides.

Now, the world does not understand such things. One of the biggest put-downs some can experience is to be found among those who don't meet certain worldy prescribed standards. They see nothing privileged in relating to others who simply don't have it economically and socially. In their thoughts Christ is divided and His Church is unequipped to handle various styles of living. The world sees nothing privileged about mingling and communicating with those who just haven't made it in this life. Conversely, there is a segment of the world that hates and envies the rich, cultured, and prominent in the Church even though they practice the Faith with concern and compassion.

How about you and me? While our lives naturally tend to be lived out at certain social and economic strata, aren't we privileged to be among those above and below? Just as we say "above and below," we are caught in the potential trap of denying the oneness in Christ that should keep us all on the same glorious and victorious spiritual plane.

Isn't the call to be single-minded with one Master, the Christ, stupendously thrilling? How privileged we are! How joyously free and healingly unrestrained we can be!

There is one more unique feature.

The fourth response is they own promise in areas that others demean unpromising.

In the Old Testament the writer of Ecclesiastes manages to give us a philosophical peek into our final point: "For everything there is a season, and a time for every matter under heaven." (3:1) He follows this with a lengthy list of life's events and their lingering significance for all. Prior to the advent, ministry, death, and resurrection of the Christ it was common for such words to end in futility and pessimism. What a difference the Savior and Lord makes! To be single-minded in His service is to cause this passage of Old Testament Wisdom Literature to be baptized in promise. Our Lord was a student of Hebrew Scripture and there is good reason to believe He was fully aware of Ecclesiastes. He moves the unpromising into the promising. We are led from the futile and pessimistic to the worthwhile and hopeful in the same areas of human existence.

From a somewhat different and yet closely related angle, our single-mindedness can and does provide for us the owning of promise for good. As someone in the public relations field has said, "If you keep turning a happening long enough, there is an interesting story someone wants to hear or see."

Under the Lordship of Christ you and I have a similar experience. The history of the Faith is sprinkled profusely with those who said "Yes, Lord" in areas while the world was snickering, hissing, and profaning. The point of view was decisive. No one can serve both God and mammon. We are appalled sometimes by the worldly attitudes in the Church that downgrade precious persons who have heard the voice of the Lord ask, "Whom shall I send, and who will go for us?" and have replied, "Here am I! Send me!"

IV.

Yes, you and I are most assuredly called to be single-minded.

There is no lack of understanding the passage in Matthew 6:24: "No one can serve two masters; for either he will hate the one and love the other, or he will be devoted to the one and despise the other. You cannot serve God and mammon."

Those who follow the call are rather easily spotted by four distinctive responses to their environment: they have power in circumstances that others are powerless; radiate purpose in situations that others find purposeless; accept privilege in circles that others consider unprivileged: and own promise in areas that others demean unpromising.

Are we willing to be different — even eccentric in the world's assessment — to live and spread the Faith? James tells us, ". . . for he who doubts is like a wave of the sea that is driven and tossed by the wind. For that person must not suppose that a double-minded man, unstable in all his ways, will receive anything from the Lord." (1:6-8) In prayerful resolve: Oh, God, we know we cannot serve two masters. We have determined today to serve One, Your Son the Christ.

CALLED TO BE SECURE
Matthew 6:25-26

I.

Underlying the struggles of today's world is the search for security.

Hustling to and fro may be legitimate ambition and an attempt to make a good living. It is, in most cases, quite possibly something else. That something else is the sheer movement of a body and mind in an attempt to feel secure. We may maintain some writers have made too much of the theme, "He doesn't know where he is going, so he doubles his speed and efforts to get there." Yet we should not deny the tip of the iceberg it evidences. The large portion of all that ice tucked below the surface is simply "insecurity" or security that cannot stand the pressures and upheavals of this life. How about you and me? Are we in a hurry for any good reason? Let's ask the more crucial and direct question: Are we hurrying forward, backward, downward, and upward just to be in motion because we cannot tolerate insecure feelings and thoughts? If we confront this inquiry, it is one with momentous healing possibilities.

The great prophet forcefully says in Jeremiah 6:14: "They have healed the sound of my people, lightly, saying, 'Peace, peace', when there is no peace." This is his reaction to people and their leaders who sought security apart from the basic lofty morality Moses and others gave them. Don't we get a glimpse of our predicament today? Have we not tended to search for security in every place but the right one and mesmerized ourselves into a flimsy, deceptive security? Jesus the Christ was also a great prophet and He places before the Christian the only security that eludes worldly measurement and control.

The Master, in His own gentle but heavily-freighted lines, says, "Therefore, I tell you, do not be anxious about your life what you shall eat or what you shall drink, nor about your body, what you shall put on. Is not life more than food, and the body more than clothing? Look at the birds of the air: they neither sow nor reap nor gather into barns, and yet your heavenly Father feeds them. Are you not of more value than they?" (Matthew 6:25-26)

He calls us to be secure. It's a strange, unwelcome kind of security, isn't it? Place food, drink, and clothing secondary? The very thought of that cuts into some pleasant appearances and thoughts, doesn't it?

You and I are called to be secure. We may not like what it entails. We cannot disown that it is the only security God ever grants to any of us. John Wesley took this call with utmost seriousness and applied it with uncanny exactness.

II.

In the text our Lord depicts the only kind of security that empowers us to live victoriously.

Christians are motivated to take the Word of the Lord into their very souls for five reasons.

III.

In the first place, it settles the question of measuring success in the accumulation of things.

The debate is over. Our Lord says His Kingdom does not measure success as the world does. If there were any doubts in the minds of His Followers or would-be followers, now they know. It must have been a hard pill for some to swallow. Undoubtedly, there were those present during the Sermon on the Mount who thought security could be found in "building more barns." Had they listened carefully, it might not have been necessary for our Lord to say it again and this time with harshness. In Luke 12:16-21, the Lord tells a parable of a rich man who prospered so that he built more and more barns and told himself that he now had ample good so it was time to take it easy, eat, drink, and be merry. Do you recall the spine-chilling end? It says: "But God said to him, 'Fool! This night your soul is required of you; and the things you have prepared, whose will they be?' So is he who lays up treasure for himself, and is not rich toward God."

Do you and I believe what He says and practice it? It is for our own good. We are called to be secure and our Lord opens the vistas necessary for us to fulfill the call. Isn't it interesting how we can quote the Bible and get good feelings until . . . all at once a dawning takes place and we are struck by the query, "Who, me?" Coming before you and me upon occasions such as this is the spiritual truth we are to allow the Word of God to penetrate the marrow of our bones. The difference in the committed and uncommitted Christian is at this very juncture. To be uncommitted is to marvel at the beauty of the text and think how nice it would look on a greeting card. To be committed is to know the beautiful change it can work internally and want to share it with others.

What is another reason Christians are motivated to take this Word from the Lord into their very souls?

In the second place, it seeks to rest in the assurance God is in charge.

"Who's in charge?" is a question we hear almost daily. Oh, it may not be phrased quite the same way each time. We like the comfort of knowing the person who heads up an organization, operation, or endeavor. For the Christian, of course, the answer is, with finality, "God is." In the workaday world that may sound remote, an evasion, or even funny. However, isn't that an integral part of our security? In fact, how do you and I even speak or think about such a thing isolated from God? An excellent way to begin each day is to proclaim, "God is in charge!" The refrain from a widely sung hymn goes:

> God will take care of you
> Through every day, o'er all the way;
> He will take care of you,
> God will take care of you.

Jesus wants you and me to know God takes care of us in uncomplicated, unexpected, and often unappreciated ways. You and I are assured about life . . . and death. He is conveying to us the eternal message that we belong to God; therefore, why be anxious? That's such a simple truth. Yet, there are times it takes nearly a lifetime for some to rest assured. Perhaps you and I just now are running the risk of what happened to an elderly man. As he was within a few hours of entering eternity, he said with sadness, regret, and yet an emerging joy, "Why didn't I believe the Sermon on the Mount the first time I read it sixty years ago, especially the part about not being anxious? Praise God, I now believe it and that's all the assurance I need." Dare you and I take a lifetime to begin believing this passage? If this is our unannounced or subconscious plan, pray that God will shake us to our cores that our deafness and blindness may be healed. John 14:27 is not appropriate just for funerals and those under heavy grief: "Peace I leave with you; not as the world gives do I give to you. Let not your hearts be troubled, neither let them be afraid." It speaks to you and me now. Rest assured; God is in charge!

There is much more to be said that flows therapeutically from Matthew 6:25-26.

In the third place, it sees the vision that this passing existence is not the end.

If all that people have here and now is the sum total of life, it would make sense to live the way most do. The world sets its time schedule in such a way that it denies anything beyond the grave, except memories for the living. It is so interesting to note that the pure materialist wherever he or she lives and under whatever national banner, is — in effect — little different from an atheistic communist. The only difference I can see is that the one worships a limited god who has planned no heaven for His children and the other serves an ideology which has no place for any god. So much of the ambitions and conquering spirit in our nation's past has been good. Nevertheless, it is a cataclysmic discovery when one is moving pell-mell towards hell and is brought to the realization this life is nearly over and eternity looms ominously.

Called to be secure on our Lord's terms is always one that puts the here and now into its proper context. It is as though our Lord is emphasizing again and again the absolute necessity of losing the desire of what the world has to offer and desiring the eternal benefits of His Kingdom. If we will listen intently, our Wesleyan heritage can teach us much about such a context. John and Charles were not men who prayed, read the Bible, and gave testimonies to the exclusion of attempts to reform abuses found in slavery, war, inhuman prisons, barbarous laws, and the liquor traffic. Their call to be secure was not worked out in lifetimes of meditating in quiet churches. Quite the contrary was true! Eternal bliss was uppermost in their minds, but the precious and priceless preliminaries to it must have careful attention.

So, we now move ahead to another reason Christians are motivated to take the text with deep seriousness and lasting appreciation.

In the fourth place it serves to point out a style of living to others.

The call to be secure puts things in rightful perspective. The Christian reverses the order of the world's priorities. The world says, "Life is filled with lollipops and you collect as many as you can as quickly as you can in any way you can wherever you can." The Christian says, "There is nothing wrong with lollipops, except they grow stale, melt under the pressure of heat, and provide very little nourishment." So many in our churches are not "bad" people. They just have never moved beyond the early stages of the Faith. I suppose no one enjoys the devouring of a lollipop more than a small child. The Letter of Paul to the Colossians records: "Him we proclaim, warning every man and teaching every man in all wisdom, that we may present every man mature in Christ." (1:28) Near the end of the same Epistle it says, "Epaphras, who is one of yourselves, a servant of Christ Jesus, greets you, always remembering you earnestly in his prayers, that you may stand mature and fully assured in all the will of God." (4:12) The way you and I live indicates whether we are still in the first grade spiritually at forty or are moving through our schooling, maturing in Christ.

While I have never been one to place much stock in a specified dress and manners code for Christians, we do well to remember two profound thoughts based in the truth of the Faith. **In The Book of Discipline of the United Methodist Church** (1976), under "The Wesleyan Perspectives in the sermons and Notes," it relates: " 'The righteousness of faith' generates its own distinctive life-style, which has been delineated best of all in Jesus' Sermon on the Mount." Then, Saint Paul points the way not only to inner change but outward manifestations as well, when he says, "Therefore, if anyone is in Christ, he is a new creation; the old has passed away, behold, the new has come." (2 Corinthians 5:17)

There is a final reason.

Christ's call to be secure allows, enables, and urges us to compare and contrast. Christians are the Body of Christ. Saint Paul says in 1 Corinthians 12:27, "Now you are the body of Christ and individually members of it." It is in this Body whose Head is Christ that you and I find our identity and unity with one another. Saint Paul says in his First Epistle: "Come to Him, to that living stone, rejected by men but in God's sight chosen and precious; and like living stones be yourselves built into a spiritual house, to be a holy priesthood, to offer spiritual sacrifices acceptable to God through Jesus Christ." (2:4-5) Who is the center and indispensable figure in our Faith? Jesus the Christ; He intends for His people to have the only security that transcends human creation, control, and curtailment.

The world groans and grasps for security by flitting here and there. It has been true since the time He walked and taught among the early believers. Philosophies come and go. Ways of life are praised and condemned. Messiahs — political, economic, social and intellectual — rise and fall. Even theological tides ebb and flow. These are the ways of the world. The eternally stable voice of the Christ is abused, confused, and refused.

Thus, we have looked upon some sharp and basic differences.

IV.

You and I hear the call to be secure.

We know it happens; it's given expression in Matthew 6:25-26: "Therefore I tell you, do not be anxious about your life, what you shall eat or what you shall drink, nor about your body, what you shall put on. Is not life more than food, and the body more than clothing? Look at the birds of the air: they neither sow nor reap nor gather into barns, and yet your heavenly Father feeds them. Are you not of more value than they?"

There are five reasons our Blessed Lord motivates us to be immersed in this passage: It settles the question of measuring success in the accumulation of things: seeks to rest in the assurance God is in charge; sees the vision that this passing existence is not the end; serves to point out a style of living to others; and sets the ways of the world over against the way Christ intends.

I want to be secure, don't you? There really isn't anything or anyone preventing it, is there? Well, then let's take the final step:

> Just as I am, thou wilt receive,
> Wilt welcome, pardon, cleanse, relieve;
> Because thy promise I believe,
> O lamb of God, I come, I come!

CALLED TO BE REPENTANT
Matthew 7:1-3

I.

Who needs to repent?

That is not a frivolous question: it is a deeply personal one. The emotions that are involved sometime remind us of fireworks on a Fourth of July. There are explosions that are tame and others that are loud. The colors are many and varied. They are mixed into blurs. I suppose there is not a single individual over eighteen who does not know such volcanic eruptions on a first-hand basis. The whole matter of repenting strikes at the very heart of our brokenness. For some the question produces a combative spirit in place of a contrite one. For others it evokes pain and panic in place of peace and pleasantries.

When you and I address the question in openness and honesty, isn't it a matter of admitting, "I need to repent, you need to repent, and so does everyone else"? The need is universal. It isn't a case of going around every day of one's life in a moping fashion. It isn't a case of repeating hourly day after day, "I'm a wicked sinner." It may not even be a situation requiring prayers of confession on a weekly basis. Nevertheless, every adult professing Christian knows while God's love is so marvelous, it is beyond full human comprehension; justice is a part of that picture. Probably the best way of all to gain a basic understanding of His love is to acknowledge that justice moves in and through it.

Yes, we all have need to repent. There are no exemptions. It is essential to coming into a right relationship with God; it is essential to continuing in that relationship. Please note I have not said where, who, how, or even what . . . only why. Praise God, an escape hatch through which all may travel is universally available!

There is a God/Man who understands our need for repentance.

In Matthew 7:1-3, He spells out, devoid of frills and ruffles, before our eyes: "Judge not, that you be not judged. For with the judgment you pronounce you will be judged, and the measure you give will be the measure you get. Why do you see the speck that is in your brother's eye, but do not notice the log that is in your own eye?" Our Lord is not angry and shouting damnation at His listeners. He is merely telling it like it is. We all have a tendency to judge. We are all prone to see specks in other's eyes while overlooking the logs in our own. What is the remedy?

We are called to be repentant. It is a call aimed at keeping us in our place. That place, of course, is in a right relationship with the God who gives us life.

II.

There are four truth-revealing assumptions of right and wrong principles in the call to be repentant. Christ bids us to recognize them.

III.

There is something wrong about us in this life.

Notice that the text is not only a declaration, it is an observation as well. Our Lord is pointing out that which exists. He does not say, "If you see the speck . . ." He says, "Why do you see the speck?" There is the clear recognition that man is not perfect or pure; he is in need of repentance. Our Lord is like that. While theologians, philosophers, and intellectuals spin and weave their thoughts, He quickly and decisively makes His point. The Christ brings us face to face with His Word and the opportunity through repentance to know the ultimate in freedom. As the Gospel of John says: ". . . If you continue in my word, you are truly my disciples, and you will know the truth, and the truth will make you free." (8:31-32)

The Lord's Word to us is another of those seemingly endless illustrations in the Bible that you and I are a part of the Fall of Man. We are always less than we should be. We are tainted by original sin. That's the reason for a crucified Savior. Jesus was and is a sacrificial offering for our sins that have an ancestral beginning with Adam. If you and I were not fallen, we have no need of a savior. God provides the means for imperfections, indeed, our sinful ways, to be continually made right or corrected. His name is above all. A hymn brings to our attention:

> Sinners, whose love can ne'er forget
> The wormwood and the gall,
> Go spread your trophies at his feet,
> And crown Him Lord of all.

It is through Him that we are not left to our own devices to save ourselves. Even though we find ourselves doing exactly that which He depicts in the text, there is a way out! It's found in the call to be repentant.

In a familiar passage, Saint Paul confesses, "I do not understand my own actions. For I do not do what I want, but I do the very thing I hate." (Romans 7:15) This is, of course, an acknowledgment of a sinful nature that always makes us less in this life than what God intends. It is at this level you and I are very much akin to the Apostle. You and I can want to be and to do the highest and the best, but we are always falling short. Satan is alive and doing well!

Thus, we conclude our initial consideration and move to contend for a second.

There is something right about the humility paving the way for repentance.

Pride is the king of vices and Satan's chief means of trapping us. The Lord recognized this in Matthew 18:3-4: "Truly, I say to you, unless you turn and become like children, you will never enter the kingdom of heaven. Whoever humbles himself like this child, he is the greatest in the kingdom of heaven." Again, in the same Gospel, He says: "He who is greatest among you shall be your servant; whoever exalts himself will be humbled, and whoever humbles himself will be exalted" (Matthew 23:11-12). We are to stay in a repentant frame of mind and temperament of heart. This enables our spirits or wills to be teachable and moldable by the Master. Deeply imbedded in the Old Testament is "Pride goes before destruction and a haughty spirit before a fall." (Proverbs 16:18) Indeed, there is something right about the humility paving the way for repentance!

Ben Franklin tells a story on himself in his **Autobiography** that typifies most of us. He says, "I conceived the bold and arduous project of arriving at moral perfection." With the aid of theology and philosophy, he listed thirteen moral virtues. For each week he listed across the top of the page a letter denoting each of the seven days. Down the left side he wrote a letter for each of the thirteen virtues. He then drew lines in red ink down the page and across so he could keep track of each infraction. After giving his readers this remarkable attempt at attaining a morally high level, he does a bit of confessing. He says:

> My list of virtues contained at first but twelve; but a Quaker friend having kindly informed me that I was generally thought proud; that my pride show'd itself frequently in

conversation; that I was not content with being in the right when discussing any point, but was overbearing, and rather insolent, of which he convinc'd me by mentioning several instances; I determined endeavouring to cure myself, if I could, of this vice or folly among the rest, and I added **Humility** to my list,

How like you and me!

Our Blessed Lord again and again in His ministry instructs His people, the Jews, to repent. In Luke, He says, ". . . unless you repent you will all likewise perish." (13:4) Why did many of them refuse to do so? An answer is given by Stephen just prior to his being stoned to death: "You stiff-necked people, uncircumcised in heart and ears, you always resist the Holy Spirit. As your fathers did, so did you." (Acts 7:51)

Now, we are going to look at a third area that saturates the text and deserves to be articulated.

There is something wrong about a superior attitude towards others.

The Christian does not consider himself better than anyone else, even the most hardened sinner. This is often difficult to practice because of the sheer joyous security that is ours. When it becomes obvious there are many who spiritually do not have what we have, it is hard not to condescend. Saint Paul relates in Romans 12:3: "For by the grace given to me I bid everyone among you not to think of himself more highly than he ought to think, but to think with sober judgment, each according to the measure of faith which God has assigned him."

How do you and I share the riches of the Faith with those never experiencing them and not take, at least, a somewhat superior attitude? The answer to that one is simply, "By the grace of God." Characteristic of this great Faith of ours is the method to convey it to others like Christians. The message and the means are inseparable portions of what Christ grants us. We are misread in our motives and misreported by others, but that is one of the necessary risks we take when we become vessels of the Master. To be rooted and grounded in the Faith is to live it, regardless of the consequences that may breed discontent, foster distrust, and produce dislocation. Matthew 10:34 refreshes our memories about such things: "Do not think that I have come to bring peace on earth; I have not come to bring peace, but a sword." If we expect life to go in its same old ruts while living the Faith, we flatly underestimate what God has given to us. A man once confessed to me that early in his walk with the Lord he was actually afraid his prayers would be answered the way he asked!

It is important you and I keep in mind in the text our Lord is especially prevailing upon those with a legalistic approach among the religious elite to repent of their ways. Spiritual blindness is never quite so extensively and heinously devastating as among those who are in the religious establishment. Our Lord is saying to religious leaders at both the lay and clergy levels, "Stay away from those hurtful tendencies to play god by judging another's spiritual state." We can and do become the kind of person Jesus mentions from time to time. The remedy is discovered in our call to be repentant.

Finally, we accept Christ's bid to recognize and accept a further point.

There is something right about leaving judgment in God's hands.

Even as we use the word "leaving," there is a hidden voice that reminds us "God is the Judge anyway." Our need, of course, is to believe and act upon the reality and finality of His judgment. The ultimate in happiness or "at-one-ment with God" is in steering clear of the ensnaring posture in life that calls for a damning and impotent legalism. In that magnificent document of American history, the Second Inaugural Address (1865), Abraham Lincoln's words pour forth with eternal relevance: ". . . as was said three thousand years ago, so still it must be said, 'The judgments of the Lord are true and righteous altogether.' " Inspired leadership in various realms of life sooner or later pay homage to the martyred President's gem of understanding.

Are you and I grateful as we "leave" judgment in His hands? Think what an awful burden it would be to have to go around taking inventory of the specks in the eyes of the others! We are not fit for the task. It belongs to God. The Christian, through repeated repentance, knows the relieving and freeing goodness of God as He takes upon Himself the judgment of His children, indeed, all persons born and unborn.

IV.

The call to be repentant must never be taken lightly.

Our Lord gives us the reason the call is constantly relevant and markedly significant: "Judge not, that you be not judged. For with the judgment you pronounce you will be judged, and the measure you give will be the measure you get. Why do you see the speck that is in your brother's eye, but do not notice the log that is in your own eye?"

There are four truth-revealing assumptions in the Word our Lord brings us: There is something wrong about us in this life; something right about the humility paving the way for repentance; something wrong about a superior attitude towards others; and something right about leaving judgment in God's hands.

We are never too good to be beyond the need of repentance.

Christians down through the ages have tended to remember this with reluctance. Then, when God does not bless us, our memories are jogged — sometimes abruptly. Often it is a simple matter of meting out judgment and not proclaiming the Gospel.

In Romans, Saint Paul begins talking about the practice of passing judgment. It is depicted as a grave matter. Then, he says a fitting, closing word to you and me: "Do you not know that God's kindness is meant to lead you to repentance?" (Romans 2:4).

CALLED TO BE ASTUTE
Matthew 7:7-8

I.

Is there an awareness or special sensitivity Christians have that others don't have?

Some would maintain that is an impossible question to answer. To be sure it is one that seems to be filled with audacity. Yet, I for one do not think it is impossible. My hesitancy comes at the point of offering proof in ways that would gain the approval and applause of the world. Into that trap, many disciples of Christ have fallen. We have said in the language and thought forms of the world here is proof we have something you don't. It has spelled disaster upon occasion. Had we only listened to the Master say: "My kingship is not of this world . . ." (John 18:36), we would not have been on the brink of disillusionment. Statistical success does not and has not always indicated documentation for our select pipeline to God. In fact, the Lord was not successful in piling up numbers. Some years ago a denominational leader said that we cannot compete with television on Sunday nights, so why bother with church services? Of course, on that narrow basis he was right. The scary part is that he thought the Body of Christ was supposed to compete with the secular extravaganzas on the tube.

You and I as Christians are select and we do have access to strength and support others do not have. That is not an egotistical statement. It is simply one of truth. Saint Paul tells the Church at Colossae: "And let the peace of Christ rule in your hearts, to which indeed you were called in the one body. And be thankful." (3:15) Saint Peter makes it emphatic: "But you are a chosen race, a royal priesthood, a holy nation, God's own people. . ." (1 Peter 2:9) Ponder that for a moment. That Scripture includes you and me!

Our Lord opens avenues to Christians unknown to non-Christians.

More specifically, in Matthew 7:7-8 He says to us: "Ask, and it will be given you; seek and you will find; knock, and it will be opened to you. For every one who asks receives, and he who seeks finds, and to him who knocks it will be opened." The fascinating glow to those words is seen in their openendedness. He doesn't indicate there are any exceptions.

Strange as it may sound, we are called to be astute. This does not mean in any way whatsoever the selfish pursuit and "success" orientation the world adores. It means: "I have been crucified with Christ; it is no longer I who live, but Christ who lives in me . . ." (Galatians 2:20)

II.

The call to be astute is one telling us to acknowledge and utilize gifts peculiarly ours.

This special relationship to God is seen in tapping truth in life's experiences, especially six.

III.

In the time of trouble we can tap truth.

In a land of affluence and a denomination of privilege we are prone to look upon trouble with disdain. The concept of sacrificial giving is foreign to our ears and perhaps has been all our lives, in or out of the Church. The very thought of giving ten percent or more of income to Christ and His Church is disruptive and cause for a whole barricade of defenses. If we can give a pittance and maintain an image of respectability before friends and "those who count," we beguile ourselves into believing we are trouble-free. The fact of the matter is, of course, the longer we refuse to confront the real situation, the more trouble we have in the long run . . . indeed, the fires of hell become more unyielding. Our denomination today bears some of the marks of the Church of England during the period John and Charles Wesley ministered. It tends again and again to serve itself in thought and deed.

From a pointedly personal standpoint, our Lord says to you and me, "Ask . . . seek . . . knock." He does not do this just to say a few well-intended words or try to appease disgruntled followers. Life says we are going to have trouble. You and I need not be engulfed by it, settling back into a state of gloom and doom. It is true, some seem to have more than their share. However, before you and I claim such mistreatment, let's be certain it isn't a case of some person or situation merely fracturing a spoiled and pampered existence. Christ has called us to ministry not minutia.

So much for initial point.

In the time of tragedy, we can tap truth.

By most and perhaps all measurements, tragedy is a factor in our lives. We anguish in pain, sorrow, and disillusionment. During these disquieting periods do we "Ask . . . seek . . . knock"? I have heard individuals say, "Pastor, I have done that but there was and is no relief." When hearing this sort of response I am reminded of the scene shortly after the Resurrection. Mary Magdelene was weeping and asked where they had taken her Lord; the greatest of all tragedies appeared to be upon her. Then the Resurrected Jesus said to her, "Woman why are you weeping? Whom do you seek?" (John 20:15) She thought He was the gardener. He was standing beside her and she did not recognize Him. When she recognized him, her relief came.

The tenacious Saint Paul had tragedy after tragedy. He says in Romans 8:18, "I consider that the sufferings of this present time are not worth comparing with the glory that is to be revealed to us." Again in Ephesians he says "Therefore take the whole armor of God, that you may be able to withstand in the evil day, and having done all to stand." (6:13) Has it occurred to you and me that we do not "stand" because we do not "Ask . . . seek . . . knock" or if we do, it is with one knee on the floor and our eyes on the clock?

We must not tarry.

In the time of triumph, we can tap truth.

While we may praise God at first for a major victory, we tend to forget His loving care. Our heads get too big. We do not know our friends. We lord it over those who are less fortunate. We are prone to bask in the sunshine of our own merits and brilliance. A string of triumphs can make us virtually blind to those about us. While we may say to ourselves, "Oh, they are just jealous," a careful examination usually reveals it is often our overbearing sense of accomplishment provoking them. On the other hand, God does not expect us to downgrade an attainment there for all to see. How, then, do we rightfully handle moments of triumph? Our Blessed Lord says "Ask . . . seek . . . knock."

The call to be astute is one which can and does make triumph a growing in grace for us and others. You and I are spiritually triumphant not because of what the world declares a triumph, but because we learn through the Master how to handle such glowing achievement. The winner in the world's sight can be a Christian and above all can manifest a Christian life at which others will marvel and — if not openly — at least secretly admire. In the world of show business, few have ever been so victoriously prominent over as long a period as Bing Crosby. I know of no one who has ever described him as arrogant, rude, or condescending . . . and that was noted long before his death. The roots of his religion ran deep. He must have found in the wellsprings of his Faith that in asking he received, in seeking he found, and in knocking it was opened to him.

Join me as we look into another common experience.

In the time of trivia, we can tap truth.

Some dear soul said, "Life has its hight points and low points but most of it is inbetween." Some of that "inbetween" seems to be trivial happenings, even boredom. What can possibly be occurring during such times that are productive for Christ and His work here on earth? Can it be that God forsakes us for a while and allows us to languish in apathetic moods with our spirits settled into drowsy neutrality? What can be good about the routine of taking two steps forward and two backwards, except that it keeps one from toppling over for having stood in the same place too long? The call to be astute is powerfully relevant in these states. We are not chosen by Christ to waste the gift of life. He lays before us the passageway of productivity even in the midst of mountains of miscellanea: "Ask . . . seek . . . knock."

Today the humdrum of living eats away in unexpected places. I am speaking, of course, of those professing the name of Jesus the Christ. Does this mean one's personal religious experience is doomed to dullness and the Master really has taken a long walk away from us? Hopefully, we know better than that. I believe feelings of useless monotony remain only as long as we refuse to "Ask . . . seek . . . knock," or because we make up our own recipe for astuteness filled with conceit and guaranteed to cure the weight of trivia on our own terms.

We tend to overlook the next event in life.

In the time of travesty, we can tap truth.

When life seems distorted, disoriented, and dislocated to the point of sheer nonsense, what do we do? Some slide into a kind of self-hypnosis that results in a dreamland, hoping their fragmentary existence can be made less harsh. Others cry out for positive threads that can give reason for life to continue. Those under the most severe strains are convinced, at least momentarily, that suicide is the only answer. If we have lived very many years at all, we know of these unwelcome states.

When life just doesn't seem to make any sense at all, what do you and I do? Are we prone to go in the directions just previously mentioned? If we do, what does our Faith have to say to us? Maybe Satan is on such a rampage; he insists to "Ask . . . seek . . . knock" is only more of the same grotesque meaninglessness. In the Gospel of John, our Lord says of the Devil, "When he lies, he speaks according to his own nature, for he is a liar and the father of lies." (8:44) The most apropos time of all to "Ask . . . seek . . . knock" is when nothing seems to make much sense and there are more loose ends than anyone can count. We are called to be astute not to outsmart the Devil on his own turf, but to enter into those supports, strengths, and answers available only to those within the Faith.

You are invited to share the last point.

In the time of tremor, we can tap truth.

Foundations shake. The expression "all hell is breaking loose" fits at different places in our lives, doesn't it? Cherished and respected people seem to come unglued. Institutions develop large cracks in them. Organizations with time-honored reputations are found to be corrupt. The institutional Church has faltered and floundered to the extremes of outright apostasy and hypocrisy. A few times in the history of the Faith the earnest acts of asking, seeking, and knocking led persons and families out of the so-called visible Church.

God has never forsaken His people, even when tremors sent things and people in all sorts of directions. He has preserved a faithful remnant all the way back to Abraham whom He told, "And I will make of you a great nation, and I will bless you, and make your name great, so that you will be a blessing." (Genesis 12:2) At the time of Jesus' Crucifixion there were many who would not have given two cents for the continuation of what He set in motion. How wrong they were! We cannot control or even accurately predict the quaking in life. Hallelujah, we have written in unerasible ink on an imperishable manuscript "Ask and receive . . . seek and find . . . knock and it will be opened!"

IV.

The call to be astute is not to be underestimated or undervalued.

The Christ opens the way: "Ask, and it will be given you; seek and you will find; knock, and it will be opened to you. For every one who asks receives, and he who seeks finds, and to him who knocks it will be opened."

Our call is seen especially in six events of the tapestry of life in which we can tap truth: in the time of trouble, tragedy, triumph, trivia, travesty, and tremor.

We have the answers to life's most basic and pressing questions.

What are we doing about it? Are we quibbling over answers that are not really answers because they are not God's? Are we wishing the Christ would sit down and explain to us every detail so that we can see if we agree? Are we thinking, "How can we manipulate something we know as Christians into an advantage for financial gain in the secular business and/or professional worlds?" If you and I are doing any of these monstrous things or something similar, may God have immediate mercy on us!

The call to be astute contains an entree into God's storehouse of riches overflowing with miracles. Let us not be deceived into believing it is our astuteness that provides and produces. To do so is to make null and void Christ's promise that to ask is to receive, to seek is to find, and to knock is to have it opened.

Our Lord's promises are true, so true in fact, they do not respond to human misuse . . . and that's a great protection built upon an eternal Faith.

CALLED TO BE PERCEPTIVE
Matthew 7:15-17

I.

Whom do we believe in this day of credibility gaps?

In recent years this has become a question of society perhaps overriding all others. It seems that sooner or later all information must have its source tested. Someone said to me recently, "Who on earth do you believe?" That was not an isolated and unique inquiry. It is one that we hear at all levels of society today. In nostalgia, some of us wish for days when a man's word was his bond. Of course, we sometimes tend to look at the past through rose-colored glasses forgetting there were then also problems of credibility. We do know that today, as never before, countless lives and even nations must daily depend on information that is not necessarily correct in every way, but is at least generally reliable.

Possibly one of the good results to come out of the quest of whom to believe is a resurgence of Bible study. The Word of God has its critics. However, it seems when those who are most interested in credible sources hit bottom, they return to the Scriptures. I suspect this is an unconscious decision by many to rely on that which is ultimate and not temporary, or that which is faithful if all other sources turn out to be less than credible. In other words, even if all sources — except the Word of God — are victimized by credibility gaps, we still have the essence of what life (and death) is all about.

We are now brought to verses aglow with basic, refreshing insight.

The Man of Galilee issues the call to be perceptive.

In Matthew 7:15-17, He gives expression to that call: "Beware of false prophets, who come to you in sheep's clothing but inwardly are ravenous wolves. You will know them by their fruits. Are grapes gathered from thorns, or figs from thistles? So, every sound tree bears good fruit, but the bad tree bears evil fruit. A sound tree cannot bear evil fruit, nor can a bad tree bear good fruit." Our Lord was pointing out to His early followers and those who were on the fringes that you have to be careful whom you believe. With a relevant ring, the first century becomes the twentieth and we are blessed by His instruction **now**.

Yes, you and I are called to be perceptive. In our sophistication, we may at first think our Lord's Word is just too simple. If that is our reaction, we better react again because what may appear to be a quiet, secondary truth is in reality a pervasive, primary truth.

II.

You and I live in a "how to" age. It seems to me our text takes us in precisely that direction. There is no reason we should back away from such a customary approach.

What are some guidelines in distinguishing between a sound tree and good fruit and a bad tree and evil fruit? We are going to use the negative "don't," but in a helpful and positive way. Join me as we continue in very practical terms.

III.

Don't be too quick to make an assessment.
Remember the Holy Spirit is not necessarily in opposition to reason and mental processes. To know trees by their fruits doesn't say a thing about turning off all brain powers and floating around on a mystical

trip. Snap judgments on any given matter sometimes get us into hot water . . . yes, even at a scalding level. While the term "spirit" carries with it a mystical connotation, we should not limit ourselves by this fact. A classic out of the Old Testament says: "Come now, let us reason together, says the Lord: though your sins are like scarlet, they shall be as white as snow; though they are red like crimson, they shall become like wool." (Isaiah 1:18) The countless, dedicated scribes and translators of the Holy Scriptures through the centuries are an excellent example of those utilizing their minds in obedience to the Holy Spirit. The Gospel of John quotes our Blessed Lord as saying, "But the Counselor, the Holy Spirit, whom the Father will send in my name, he will teach you all things, and bring to your remembrance all that I have said to you." (14:26)

Impatience, especially in the area of which Christ is speaking in the text, can be the Christian's most besetting sin. Maybe the fruit is in our favorite color and we immediately are persuaded the fruit is good. Then we discover on closer examination the appealing color covers a very sour, even bitter, fruit. Maybe the fruit is glistening in the brightness of a summer sun and its luster causes drivers to stop and pick it. Then, as it is being placed on the car seat, a slight imperfection is detected and a few miles down the road a worm makes an appearance. A pocketknife discloses a substantial section is rotten. Today patience works wonders in a world not easily impressed. You and I are to take a second look, yes, even a third and fourth look.

What's another practical pointer?

Don't be too critical.

Sometimes you and I look for the perfect tree and the perfect fruit. For a generation or so this seems to be particularly true in the area of mass evangelism and revival meetings. Some of this is overreaction which seems to have been ignited when the novel **Elmer Gantry** began to have a wide reading. To be sure there were and are charlatans or those in sheep's clothing who were and are inwardly ravenous wolves. Not only does some fruit rot, the tree becomes a despicable eyesore and innumerable persons end up with a terrific tummy ache. Such abuse is commonly known. However, let's ask a sobering question: Are the critics of such disreputable, mobile preachers to be allowed to fix a mindset against all such persons in mass evangelism? Let's not be too critical as we taste and test the message. The redeeming Word of Christ comes to us in a myriad of forms, none of them perfect.

The revelation that Billy Graham and associates have a multi-million dollar fund the public knew nothing about has sent shock waves into some homes around the country. I am not sure why some have been so surprised. Personally, I see no indication of scandal. Billy Graham may have made a mistake by not making a full and complete financial statement available to the public long ago. However, let's not be too critical; Billy is neither God incarnate nor the only means to save souls. Some seem to have believed he was both prior to the mentioned disclosure. Let's appreciate the man as a blessed but imperfect instrument of God.

The next guideline may be the most difficult to recognize and practice.

Don't be led easily to conclusions others have decided.

A story is told of George Washington Carver, the greatest Negro agricultural chemist. You may recall he was born of slave parents and was illiterate until he was almost twenty years old. At any rate, it is said he asked God what secrets the peanut contained. God responded by telling him to go find out for himself. Mr. Carver took direction. From the peanut and sweet potato he developed more than a hundred different products, including plastics, lubricants, medicines, and face creams. Doesn't God deal that way with you and me?

Do we allow others to do our thinking for us? If someone says, "That's a bad tree and you won't like the fruit at all," do we bother to check it out. Perhaps the reverse case is presented for our quick concurrence: that's a good tree and you will like the fruit. Do Christians actually permit this to happen to them? It would appear there are times when they do. Once in a while this causes a church leader, lay or clergy, more than a modicum of chagrin. Others have decided on the integrity of so-and-so leader and you are expected to fall in line. Do you and I succumb sometimes without even knowing it? That isn't a flattering thought, is it? In fact that borders on downright humiliation. It hardly needs to be mentioned that a clergyman is foisted at times into a position of re-selling persons who have previously been sold a negative bill of goods. Of course, there is the tendency for laity to know one another better than even the clergyman suspects. That can be a very positive and enlightening state of affairs!

Let's probe still further.

Don't be afraid of hard work in getting answers.

Our call to be perceptive isn't one punctuated by magic wands and ouija boards. If we are to know the facts, we must be willing to mine them. Perception is sometimes much like the often quoted definition of genius, "99% perspiration and 1% inspiration." We have to scrape away and dig deeper. Shortcuts may only cause short circuits. Astrological tables are fascinating and provide coincidences on a scale that is in some instances an awesome encounter. Yet, they break down at the crux of the problem of spiritual credibility; they can supply neither personal Savior nor Lord.

The line of least resistance or a minimum of work to acquire answers is typical of many. It's even said by some sociologists and psychologists a group may be leaning in one direction of action and two percent of it will boldly decide with firmness on the opposite, thereby causing the entire group to shift, largely because conflict is just too troublesome and draining. What does that say about the potential of a handful of dedicated ravenous wolves who pose as innocent, harmless sheep? Our Lord wants us to put laziness aside when it comes to perceiving integrity. We must seek to know if a source is credible by studying both its being and the results or products of that being. Will there be assistance other than our natural ability and energy? Of course there will. For the Christian, the Holy Spirit is present and that will probably have nothing to do with the gift of speaking in tongues! The Christ says the Father, "Will give you another Counselor, to be with you forever, even the spirit of truth, whom the world cannot receive, because it neither sees him nor knows him; you know him, for he dwells with you, and will be in you." (John 14:16-17)

There is a fifth and final tool that has the effect of completing an underlying sequence.

Don't be timid in expressing what is really felt and thought.

In Paul's second letter to Timothy, he says, "For God did not give us a spirit of timidity but a spirit of power and love and self-control." (1:7) Not to speak up in situations where credibility is at stake might be a grievous, criminal act. As is so often the case, it is our refusal to do what we know is right that gets us and others in trouble. Of course, we are not speaking of blabbermouths who have expert opinions on everyone and everything. I can almost hear Christ say as we bring this up: "Indeed, they have their reward." The Christian has power, love, and self-control. To have such gifts is to lay timidity aside. To do so is not to forsake humility, for the humble person can be the most vocal and forth-right of all under the inspiration of God.

Our own credibility as members of the Body of Christ suffers when we do not say what we mean and mean what we say. If a Christian cannot be believed or will not speak out, what hope does a dying and sinful world have? You and I may be wrong from time to time, but so what? This is only a colossal opportunity to show others we are not threatened by the possibility of being wrong and are willing, if need be, to make amends. Our perceptions cannot always be foolproof. We may have to back off, but so what? In the Love Chapter, Saint Paul unfolds for us these words: "Love is patient and kind; love is not jealous or boastful; it is not arrogant or rude. Love does not insist on its own way . . ." (1 Corinthians 13:4-5) We all have to learn that for Christ to dwell in us is not to make us free from error, but it is an indwelling that keeps us moving in right directions.

IV

Called to be perceptive makes the difference in whether you and I are deceived by the disreputable ridden with evil or blessed by integrity saturated with goodness.

That masterful Teacher, our Master, lays His Word before us: "Beware of false prophets, who come to you in sheep's clothing but inwardly are ravenous wolves. You will know them by their fruits. Are grapes gathered from thorns, or figs from thistles? So, every sound tree bears good fruit, but the bad tree bears evil fruit. A sound tree cannot bear evil fruit, nor can a bad tree bear good fruit."

Our guidelines for the purpose of distinguishing are childlike in their simplicity: don't be too quick to make an assessment; too critical; led easily to

142

conclusions others have decided; afraid of hard work
in getting answers; and timid in expressing what is
really felt and thought.

So, we have followed a pragmatic "how . to"
approach, but the call to be perceptive comes from
the eternal Christ. Isn't this typical of our Faith? It isn't
just theory, ideals, and nice words. It is profoundly
down-to-earth, basic, and redeemingly practical.

John, the Apostle of Love, said, years after the
Resurrection, to his people and now to us, "Beloved,
do not believe every spirit, but test the spirits to see
whether they are of God; for many false prophets
have gone out into the world. By this you know the
Spirit of God: every spirit which confesses that Jesus
Christ has come in the flesh is of God, and every spirit
which does not confess Jesus is not of God." (1 John
4:1-3)

CALLED TO BE HONEST
Matthew 7:21-23

I.

Claiming something we don't have can be very troublesome, even calamitous.

Rank dishonesty with oneself, let alone those around us, creates tumult. What does it do to you, me, and others to be dishonest? I'm not speaking of gray areas where there is a chance of misunderstanding. I'm speaking of those areas where the person is dishonest to the point of living a lie. We are mentally healthy, as Howard J. Clinebell, Jr. says, as we are "able to see reality — the world and other people — with accuracy because (our) subjective needs do not distort (our) perceptions." This is not to free us from anxiety and tensions. It is in the highest and best sense to say that to keep us honest with ourselves, especially in that prison which would have us make claims that are unreal, is of paramount importance in mental health. While we all like to create our own fanciful worlds from time to time, we had best know that is what we are doing. To pray "Oh, Lord, shield and save me from the consequences of my living" is the prayer not so much of the pagan as of those thoroughly dishonest with themselves. Shakespeare must have been truly inspired in **Hamlet** Act I, Scene iii, when he says:

This above all: to thine own self be true,
And it must follow, as the night the day,
Thou canst not then be false to any man.

It is in the corridors of our minds and the reservoirs of our hearts that honesty must gain a full and complete hearing.

As children we were Napoleon, Babe Ruth, Mickey Mantle, Queen Elizabeth, or Judy Garland. Have we allowed the natural fantasies of childhood to pervade our adult lives? Are we now making claims that have no substance in fact, but we are afraid of a painful revelation that a thorough-going honesty might inflict? A face-lift at fifty may make one look thirty-five. Does that change chronological and biological fact? To be and live among the gods as a child, if it becomes a fixed form as an adult, leads one only to great embarrassment and perhaps wreaks havoc in one's life and others.

Jesus the Christ was well-acquainted with people who made claims that were not theirs to make.

We are called by Him to be honest.

In Matthew 7:21-23, He deals with the matter: "Not every one who says to me, 'Lord, Lord!' shall enter the kingdom of heaven but he who does the will of my Father who is in heaven. On that day many will say to me, 'Lord, Lord, did we not prophesy in your name, and cast out demons in your name, and do many mighty works in your name?' And then will I declare to them, 'I never knew you; depart from me, you evil doers.' " While this may sound far more spiritually important than our opening remarks, I doubt that it is. There is a distinct call to you and me to be honest in our relationships with God and man.

Satan will sometimes mislead us gently by telling us such-and-such a passage in the Bible just doesn't apply to us!

II.

The call requires a continual looking into an unbiased mirror with a cross and an empty tomb in the background. Such a mirror is capable of quickly showing a trio of blemishes.

III.

The first of the trio is fakery in the name of God.

It is said in the world of the occult all sorts of superhuman things take place. Stories that come out of Africa, South America, and our own continent are bizarre and seem to be dyed deeply with wickedness. It is not only among the illiterate tribes and snake-infested jungles we find such forces at work. It is found as well among the well-read, who have the latest in conveniences modernity can offer. Sooner or later I am told much of this calls on the name of God or in the name of the gods for success. Some happenings are so astounding that believers are made and a kind of status attained. Of course, the world of which we are speaking is, for the most part, not new.

Isaiah of the Old Testament denounced magic and a people's bent to be beguiled by those claiming the ability to divine truth. In Isaiah 8:19, the Prophet says, "And when they say to you, 'Consult the mediums and the wizards who chirp and mutter,' should not a people consult their God? Should they consult the dead on behalf of the living?" Some were relying on peeping wizards and muttering soothsayers. Such strains of fakery moved from generation to generation so that in our Lord's time He dealt with forms of the same thing that were merely more perfected.

The Master, upon making a blind and dumb demoniac speak and see, was confronted by the Pharisees. They claimed Jesus could cast out demons only in the name of Beelzebul, the prince of demons, or Satan. His response bears a close relationship to the text as He says, ". . .if it is by the Spirit of God that I cast out demons, then the kingdom of God has come upon you." In those days Satan could ascend to the place of God in some minds and our Lord must have been well aware of this. Note that He says, "by the Spirit of God that I cast out demons."

Perhaps the most interesting of all New Testament stories about this hellish problem is found in Acts 19:11-20. The author of Acts tells his readers that extraordinary miracles were performed by God through Paul. Handkerchiefs or aprons were carried away from his body to the sick; diseases left them and evil spirits came out of them. Not wanting a good thing to get away, itinerant Jewish exorcists decided to use the name of the Lord Jesus to cause evil spirits to flee from bodies containing them. The result of their attempt is one of the most captivating you will read. It says the evil spirit knows Jesus and Paul but not the exorcists, who are further identified as the seven sons of the Jewish high priest. Then the man who has the evil spirit overpowers them, causing them to flee out of the house naked and wounded. The word was circulated as to what had happened and those professing the Christ confessed their practices. Those who practiced magic arts brought their books, valued at 50,000 pieces of silver, together and burned them before witnesses. The passage closes by telling us, "So the word of the Lord grew and prevailed mightily."

Are you and I influenced and controlled by such fakery?

The second of the trio is deception in the name of facesaving.

Have we now entered an arena too distant from what our Lord had in mind in the text? I hardly think so. In the nittygritty of life we may deceive in order to save face. In the call to be honest, it is at this very elementary level we may have the most difficulty. If we can spend time and energy dealing with those fakers who misuse in the name of God, we can begin to feel rather well about our present state of salvation. After all, who among us is going out today with evil intent to prophesy, cast out demons, and do mighty works in the name of God? Our little games and game plans to save face seem trite by comparison. Of course, that is likely what Satan wants us to think. When we hear the words, "I never knew you; depart from me, you evil doers," it sounds as though they are directed at persons damning themselves and others by dastardly deeds with gargantuan doses of deceit. You and I know the truth at hand, don't we?

There is nothing quite so grossly grotesque as unbridled pride. Men, women, and youth have been known to stop at nothing to avoid the exposure that truth brings. Murders have been committed. Pain has been inflicted on generations. Hate has disregarded the Master's wooing of the message of love. The promise of freedom is replaced by the bondage of preserving a self that sooner or later must die. Jealousy steals away the impulse to crush the barriers that have produced nothing but threatening overtones born of deceitfulness. A greedy and inflated self charms the unsuspecting and makes a mockery of warm, open human relationships. Snakes of unrelenting egotism hiss at those who could and are willing to help. Precious human beings waste and rot away in prisons of pride. A moment of trying disclosure is rejected in favor of mountains of dishonesty.

Our Lord speaks of "the will of my Father" and this should be clue enough for you and me. We cannot do His will encased in shells of pride. We cannot really play hide-and-seek with God! The person going through life saving face has no sense of the loving gratitude every converted sinner enjoys. We may not go through life like the proverbial "bull in a china shop;" we may very well protect all the china from breakage, only to learn too late we have preserved that which should have been broken into a million pieces years ago.

The call to be honest demands we ask, "Are you and I deceivers in the name of face-saving?

The third of the trio is insincerity in the name of social acceptance.

"I'll be whatever I have to be, just to fit in" is an ever-present attitude. It seems to me the call to be honest demands that Christians say a word of warning. We all like to belong. No one wants to be an outsider. No one likes the stigma of "being out of the group." We all like to feel comfortable. The pressures of society have told us to believe one of the ultimates in life is to be acceptable, feel comfortable, and be part of a group. Our youth know these pressures only too well. In fact, aren't they taught in numerous ways to be insincere in order to be socially acceptable? What we need to remind all ages is that we can go to hell in a group just as easily — perhaps more easily — as we can separately. The Devil is such a brilliantly subtle creature upon occasions!

As we move through various times with lives coming and going, certain passages of Scripture are more germane than others. There is one that should be written on our hearts and firmly implanted in our minds during this decade and, I strongly suspect, for the remainder of the century. I am speaking of a single verse in Paul's theological masterpiece, his letter to the Romans. In 12:2 he says, "Do not be conformed to this world but be transformed by the renewal of your mind, that you may prove what is the will of God, what is good and acceptable and perfect." That does not say to be hermits, to flaunt one's eccentricities, or to be a one-person revolutionary taking the ax to all social relationships. It does call us to be honest to the Faith, in particular the Christ who died for us and arose again. My friends and co-workers in Christ, there are groupings into which we will not fit. Insincerity just to get in borders on being blasphemous, that is, showing contempt for our Lord and Savior. Do you think He was suitably fitted and found to be well adjusted among many of the Roman and Jewish social groupings? Heavens, no! He stuck out like a sore thumb! Had He accomodated Himself to their mores He most likely would not have been crucified ... and that just may say something about your religious experience and mine.

As for those who criticize us for having two left feet and posing a threat to their own carefully sanctioned modes of behavior, we should quote the late E. Stanley Jones. He regarded his critics as "the unpaid guardians of my soul." He heard clearly and lived by the call to be honest. It was not only at the level of prophesying, casting out demons, and doing mighty works. It was also at the level of out-and-out insincerity to gain social acceptance.

To our last point we must hasten to add that holiness or spiritual wholeness treats such insincerity as a malignancy to be promptly removed in its entirety.

IV.

You and I are called to be honest, and in areas we may be slow to recognize.

Our Lord comes at us at a level deserving continual pondering: "Not every one who says to me, 'Lord, Lord,' shall enter the kingdom of heaven, but he who does the will of my Father who is in heaven. On that day many will say to me, 'Lord, Lord, did we not prophesy in your name, and cast out demons in your name, and do many mighty works in your name?' And then will I declare to them, 'I never knew you; depart from me, you evil doers.'"

An unbiased mirror with a cross and empty tomb in the background tells us to be on the lookout for a trio of blemishes: fakery in the name of God; deception in the name of face-saving; and insincerity in the name of social acceptance.

The apex or highest point of hypocrisy is claiming the Christ in our lives when He is not present: the nadir or lowest point of disgrace is when the Christ says, "I never knew you; depart from me, you evil doers."

Our Lord emerged from a magnificent religion, but many had fallen victim to the enticements of fakery, deception, and insincerity. To such a condition He says in Matthew 23:25, "Woe to you, scribes and Pharisees, hypocrites! for you cleanse the outside of the cup and of the plate, but inside they are full of extortion and rapacity." You pray for me and I'll pray for you — indeed, let's all **pray** for one another — **that we will not be disowned on that day which dwarfs all others.**

CALLED TO BE OBEDIENT
Matthew 7:24-27

I.

Every great and redeeming movement of the Church is given birth and direction by obedience.

The New Testament has examples galore. The Saints, Peter and Paul, were God-intoxicated and this reflected especially in their obedience to God through Christ. Very early in the life of the Church the apostles were told by the high priest not to teach in the name of Jesus. In Acts 5:29 we discover "But Peter and the apostles answered, 'We must obey God rather than men.'" Paul begins his letter to the Romans by describing himself as a "servant (or slave) of Jesus Christ."

Saint Augustine's early life was marred by desires for sex, power, and money. His conversion led him to a disciplined life that sought to do the will of God totally and completely. In his **Confessions** he says, "This only I know that woe is me except in Thee: not only without but within myself also; and all abundance, which is not my God, is emptiness to me."

Martin Luther "stuck by his guns." It was dangerous for him to disagree openly and firmly with the institutional Church of his day. He obeyed his God when he said to the papal powers, "Here I stand: I cannot do otherwise. God help me!"

John Calvin was a frail and sickly man. Once committed to a task, as he understood obedience to God, he attacked it ferociously. He often labored twelve to eighteen hours a day. He gave to us the concept of the sovereignty of God which remains unsurpassed.

John Wesley was obedient to his God to the point of being offensively rigid and a turncoat to his religious tradition in the eyes of many. Typical of the man is a brief sentence from one of his prayers: "I give thee myself and my all." It was in obedience to his God he spent sixty years preaching, teaching, organizing, and administering.

In this century, among our Roman Catholic friends there arose a Pope by the name of John XXIII. That part of the Church will never again be the same. Doors and windows were not only opened; they were opened widely. He was to have been a transitional Pontiff! He gave all who profess the name of Christ opportunity to stand together in Christ. I, for one, do not doubt his obedience to his God.

Our Blessed Lord comes to the end of the Sermon on the Mount and gives us a concluding word.

In Matthew 7:24-27, He calls you and me to be obedient: "Every one then who hears these words of mine and does them will be like a wise man who built his house upon the rock; and the rain fell, and the floods came, and the winds blew and beat upon the house, but it did not fall, because it has been founded on the rock. And everyone who hears these words of mine and does not do them will be like a foolish man who built his house upon the sand; and the rains fell, and the floods came, and the winds blew and beat against that house, and it fell; and great was the fall of it."

We are now brought to terms with what makes us Christians, keeps us Christians, and enables us to grow in the Faith.

II.

To be specific, the Master calls for obedience to those disciplines which are an indispensable part of the **hearing and doing of His Word.**

He is speaking of a two-fold style of living, one mostly passive and the other largely active; one receives or inhales the spirit of God and the other gives or exhales the spirit of God.

How then do we hear and do His Word?

III.

"To Hear" His Word means to be obedient, at least, to three discplines.

The **first** is study, especially the Bible.

One of the major revelations to some biblically-oriented laity and clergy is the lack of elementary information of the Bible on the part of numerous Church members. This means there are those quoting other sources, claiming it comes from the Bible. It also means there are misquotations. Countless numbers have not taken the Word of God into their beings because they simply do not study it. Surveys have shown that a youth confirmation class after a few weeks of instruction knows more about the Bible than many of their parents. This sort of illiteracy is a betrayal of the Protestant Reformation.

One of the sure characteristics of near death is a large body of persons who either ignore regular and systematic Bible study or poke fun at those who do read and study with care. There are certain phases of our Faith that can be labeled out-and-out conservative. By that I mean Bible study is not optional for the Christian. A liberal may say take it or leave it. Such a person is wrong and, sadly, will likely lead others down a primrose path dotted with attractive but dying flowers and shrubs. The Word of God comes to us from "the Book" and to drink deeply from it is "to hear" His Word.

The **second** is preaching.

Preaching is a sacramental act. In other words, it is a means God uses to bring us in touch with His grace. This means it is not just another speech or form of public address. It is a specific time when preacher and congregation interact together. For the laity, it is a serious matter of hearing. For the preacher, it is a serious matter of proclaiming the Word of God with all the tools available.

Perhaps the best known definition of preaching was given to us by Phillips Brooks, that great pulpiteer of the last century in the Episcopal Church. He said "Preaching is truth through personality." I do not, as some, feel this is an outdated definition. If we preachers shy away from it, it seems to me we do so because we do not like the awesome responsibility placed upon us. Some have found in recent years it is more satisfying and acceptable to spend long hours in counseling and administration with a de-emphasis on preaching. Sorry, I'm with Phillips Brooks who gave himself with little thought of time to preparing and preaching sermons, while still finding time to pastor and administer.

Sermons are prepared to be heard and hopefully to be read in many cases. FOR THE LAITY TO ENTER a sanctuary unprepared to listen is two strikes against any well-planned, inspiring sermon. Copies of sermons are extensions of what has been conveyed verbally. They are not emergency measures to give to those who prefer to be present only physically in worship or not at all. The printed word is intended in a way for those who want to finish what the preacher has already started verbally. In a sense it is a continued hearing of the proclaimed and elaborated Word.

Preaching through the ages has had and, I believe continues to have, an intangible quality about it, which in essence means only God can make it a blessing. Scholarship alone cannot determine the success or failure of a sermon. Literary expertise alone cannot make it effective in bringing persons to Christ. Theological training alone cannot cause it to be God's Word for that occasion. Homiletical refinement alone cannot demand and get God's blessing. While preaching may appear to be a means for a person to dominate, entertain, and satisfy desires for appearing before a group, it is probably the most humble act the pastor is called to do. To give his people less than his relationship to God as their pastoral leader requires, places him in jeopardy under the judgment of God. There is an integrity of preaching that cannot be compromised. If it is, hell becomes more than just a word receiving ridicule in our day. It becomes a place of estrangement from God, deserved and filled with torment.

The **third** is prayer.

While praying to God may cause hundreds and even thousands of words to fall from our lips, it is still a matter of our hearing that "still small voice." It is an experience of inhaling His spirit. We do not force God with our many words and phrases to do anything or to refrain from an act. You and I are the recipients.

In the poem "The Passing of Arthur," in the series **Idylls of the King,** Tennyson says, "More things are wrought by prayer than this world dreams of." And so it is true! When His children pour out their deepest longings and concerns, God does not fail us.

When our Lord gave us His model prayer, note that after the initial adoration to God and the pleas for submission to His will, it calls upon God to act. The words are "give," "forgive," and "lead." We can almost hear in the background Isaiah's words: "but they who wait for the Lord shall renew their strength, they shall mount up with wings like eagles, they shall run and not be weary, they shall walk and not faint." (40:31)

So, the call to be obedient in hearing His Word is spelled out for us in three specific disciplines.

Let's look at the second aspect of the two-fold style of living.

"To do" His word likewise means to be obedient, at least, to three disciplines.

The **first** is daily, almost routine, service to and for one another.

The Apostle Paul sounds the keynote as he says, "Let love be genuine; hate what is evil, hold fast to what is good; love one another with brotherly affection; outdo one another in showing honor." (Romans 12:10-11) This is the Apostle's way of emphasizing the living out of our Faith as we relate to persons on a daily basis. Perhaps your reaction is one of "Well, that's no big deal," and you are right. It is a rightful expectation for all who profess the name of Christ. We cannot play the part of a chameleon changing colors that cause us to be Christians only as the situation seems to demand. It is the consistency of our lives as they are lived with and before others that the "doing of our Faith" rises or falls, is implemented or thwarted. This is just as true in our era as it was for the Church at Rome in Paul's time.

It is in giving ourselves away and exhaling the spirit of God we are doers. The Epistle of James lays it squarely on the line in 1:22: "But be doers of the word, and not hearers only, deceiving yourselves." This is really a building upon what our Lord says in the text: "... who hears these words of mine and does them ..." It is in our doing that sinners are made to see and feel their need of the Savior and Lord who gave Himself without reservation.

The **second** is financial support of both the local church and the Church Universal.

Money represents a person. How he or she spends it tells with clarity where his or her priorities are. A veteran of the ministry told me the best way to know what a person considers important is upon his or her death to take, if available, all cancelled checks of the years and scrutinize them. If that were to happen to you and me upon our demise, how would we look to posterity? Would we be considered doers of His Word? Indeed, what people do with their money tells a great deal about them! A common phrase today is, "You are what you eat;" we might hasten to add, "You are also what you spend your money for." God has no need to run a tape on our giving habits, but we should, at least, annually and with eyes not jaundiced by an unforgiving spirit and warped by using money as a tomahawk.

The **third** is sacrificial example.

Isaiah speaks of Christ as being the "suffering servant." "He was despised and rejected by men; a man of sorrows, and acquainted with grief; and as one from whom men hide their faces he was despised, and we esteemed him not." (Isaiah 53:3) You and I, like it or not and admit it or not, are also sacrificial servants.

To do His Word has meant sacrifice for an unbroken chain of Christians since those vibrant, unforgettable days of the Church's birth. Many have died and are dying for their Faith. Would you and I? Do we know the nail prints, bleeding side, crown of thorns, and mocking from the crowd are an ever present part of an eternal Faith . . . to which you and I have sworn allegiance?

So, the call to be obedient in doing His Word is spelled out for us in three specific disciplines.

IV

As we conclude our labor of love in the greatest of all sermons, we are called first, foremost, and finally to be obedient.

The Christ of the Ages provides us with the Word that makes or breaks the Sermon on the Mount in our lives: "Every one then who hears these words of mine and does them will be like a wise man who built his house upon the rock; and the rain fell, and the floods came, and the winds blew and beat upon the house, but it did not fall, because it had been founded on

158

the rock, and every one who hears these words of mine and does not do them will be like a foolish man who built his house upon the sand; and the rains fell, and the floods came, and the winds blew and beat against that house, and it fell; and great was the fall of it."

The hearing of His Word is found especially in study, preaching, and prayer; the doing of His Word is found especially in daily service, financial support, and sacrificial example.

The Sermon on the Mount is a manual for growing in the grace of our Savior and Lord; it is given power in love by the call to be obedient.

You and I are privileged beyond all worldly measurement. We can and do receive or inhale and give or exhale the Spirit of the Living God. Indeed, "How great thou art, how great thou art!"